FROM BRYCGSTOW TO BRISTOL IN 45 BRIDGES

crossing each one only once

Photography and text by Jeff Lucas

Bristol Books CIC, The Courtyard, Wraxall, Wraxall Hill, Bristol, BS48 1NA

From Brycgstow To Bristol In 45 Bridges
Written and researched by Jeff Lucas

Photography by Jeff Lucas

The original concept of solving The Königsberg Bridge Problem
for Bristol was devised and researched by Dr Thilo Gross.

Published by Bristol Books 2019

ISBN: 9781909446182

Copyright: Jeff Lucas / Bristol Books

Design: Joe Burt

Jeff Lucas has asserted his rights under the Copyright, Designs and Patents Act of 1988 to be identified as the author of this work.

All rights reserved. This book may not be reproduced or transmitted in any form or in any means without the prior written consent of the publisher, except by a reviewer who wishes to quote brief passages in connection with a review written in a newspaper or magazine or broadcast on television, radio or on the internet.

A CIP record for this book is available from the British Library.

Supported by:
University of BRISTOL

CONTENTS

Introduction by Jeff Lucas   5
Foreword by Professor Alan Champneys, University of Bristol   7
Map   8
The Bridges
    1. Bristol Bridge   11
    2. St Philip's Bridge   13
    3. Castle Ditch Bridge   17
    4. Temple Bridge   20
    5. Valentine's Bridge   22
    6. Meads Reach Bridge   24
    7. 8. Bath Bridges (East and West)   27
    9. Brock's bridge   29
    10. St Philip's Footbridge   33
    11. Temple Meads Relief Line Bridge   36
    12. Sparke Evans Park Bridge   38
    13. 14. St Philips Causeway Bridges (East and West)   41
    15. Barton Hill Bridge   45
    16. Netham Lock Bridge (East)   47
    17. New Brislington Bridge   50
    18. St Anne's Footbridge   52
    19. Netham Lock Bridge (West)   47
    20. Feeder Canal Footbridge   55
    21. Marsh Bridge   59
    22. Totterdown Bridge   62
    23. Langton St Bridge (Banana Bridge)   65
    24. 25. Bedminster Bridges (East and West)   69
    26. Bathurst Basin Footbridge   71
    27. 28. Bathurst Basin Roadbridges (East and West)   74
    29. Gaol Ferry Bridge   77
    30. Vauxhall Bridge   79
    31. Ashton Avenue Bridge   81
    32. Avon Bridge   84
    33. South Entrance Lock Bridge   88
    34. South Entrance Lock Walkway   91
    35. Plimsoll Bridge   92
    36. Clifton Suspension Bridge   96
    37. Avonmouth Road Bridge   101
    38. Portway Viaduct   106
    39. Pooles Wharf Bridge   108
    40. North Junction Lock Bridge   112
    41. South Junction Lock Bridge   115
    42. Prince Street Bridge   117
    43. Pero's Bridge   121
    44. Redcliffe Bridge   123
    45. Castle Bridge   127
The Königsberg Bridge Problem by Dr Thilo Gross   130
Bristol's Waterways – A Very Brief History   136
Walk Instructions   138
Bibliography & Acknowledgements   144

JEFF LUCAS

Jeff read sciences at the University of Leicester and obtained a masters degree in geochemistry at Leeds in 1974. He lived in Bristol for 25 years before moving to Portishead, after retirement from a career in occupational health and safety. He is a long-standing member of Bristol Civic Society and was the events organiser for several years. He has led walking tours through various parts of the city for the Society.

He is a keen amateur photographer. His work has been shown in the Royal West of England Academy Open Exhibition, he has received a commendation in the Sony World Photography Awards and was a prizewinner in the "24 hours in Bristol" competition. He regularly exhibits his photographs as a founder member of the Portishead Arts group of artists. He is married and has two cats.

INTRODUCTION

This book is composed of the individual stories of the 45 bridges that span Bristol's main waterways which can be crossed on foot. They illuminate many key aspects of the 1,000 year history of the city. The bridges are linked into a 45km walk which is a solution to a quirky puzzle which eventually had a huge significance in mathematics — how to cross a given set of bridges *crossing each one only once*. The puzzle was first propounded and solved nearly 300 years ago in Königsberg (now called Kaliningrad), hence the name The Königsberg Bridge Problem.

A few years ago my attention was caught by a short article in the Bristol Post relating that a maths lecturer at Bristol University had solved The Königsberg Bridge Problem for the (then) 43 bridges of Bristol. Intrigued by this I contacted the academic in question, Dr Thilo Gross, who gave me permission to write a longer article and draw a proper map of the walk for the Bristol Civic Society Magazine where it was duly published.

That article has now been expanded into the book that is before you. Thilo has provided a new solution to the "Problem" to take account of two new bridges which have necessitated a completely new route.

With the current number and location of the bridges the walk is fortuitously circular, so you can start and finish at a point of your own choosing. I chose to begin the book at Bristol Bridge, the city's point of origin, which means, very neatly, that you finish the walk at one of Bristol's newest bridges, Castle Bridge. I ask your forbearance for a little repetition of facts in different chapters to take account of those who start at a location other than Bristol Bridge.

Before you start, it might be helpful to read the short chapter on the history and layout of Bristol's waterways (page 136.)

I hope you will enjoy exploring Bristol in this new and unusual way. This walk will take you into strange and not-so-strange places where you will discover the delightful and the dreadful.

In everyday life we rarely pay attention to bridges but they are vital to human society and its history. They are of significance economically and socially. They are strategically important in warfare — battles are fought over them. They constitute powerful imagery in literature and poetry. They can be as simple as a plank, but also superlative feats of design and engineering. They are often the primary subject of visual art, and can be sculptural objects in their own right.

Take the time to explore the bridges. Go down to the water — look underneath and from the sides — this is often where most interest is found. I hope you will be spurred on to make detours and extensions, and to find out more about the history, the development, and the complex layers of life of the city of Bristol. This book is also my personal homage to a great city that was my home for 25 years.

Jeff Lucas

" The bridge swings over the stream with ease and power. It does not just connect banks that are already there. The banks emerge as banks only as the bridge crosses the stream. The bridge causes them to lie across from each other. One side is set off against the other by the bridge. Nor do the banks stretch along the stream as indifferent border strips of the dry land. With the banks, the bridge brings to the stream the one and the other expanse of the landscape lying behind them. It brings stream and bank and land into each other's neighborhood. *The bridge gathers the earth as landscape around the stream.* Thus it guides and attends the stream through the meadows. Resting upright in the stream's bed, the bridge–piers bear the swing of the arches that leave the stream's waters to run their course. The waters may wander on quiet and gay, the sky's floods from storm or thaw may shoot past the piers in torrential waves — the bridge is ready for the sky's weather and its fickle nature. Even where the bridge covers the stream, it holds its flow up to the sky by taking it for a moment under the vaulted gateway and then setting it free once more. "
Martin Heidegger, "*Building, Dwelling, Thinking*"

FOREWORD

It is my pleasure on behalf of the University of Bristol to write a foreword to this beautiful book. My erstwhile colleague Dr Thilo Gross is really a singular individual. He is a leading international expert on the theory of networks; that is, if you like, the global interconnectedness of everything. Among other things, he has applied these ideas to ecology, industrial supply chains, voting patterns and to city demographics. We feel honoured that for eight years he chose to make Bristol his home.

Thilo has an intense attitude to life. Often surviving on very little sleep, he has periods of extreme academic productivity. He approaches hobbies similarly. After arriving in Bristol he discovered a love of walking. Not necessarily hiking in the beautiful rural West-country, but just walking. Walking along familiar trails from his flat, around the streets of Bristol, and beyond. Hundreds of miles a week.

Then he hit upon an idea. Leonhard Euler (1707–1783) is thought to be the most prolific mathematician ever to have lived. The origins of network theory can be traced to Euler's solution to a famous walking puzzle. In the city of Königsberg, a port city with similarities to Bristol, the gentry liked to promenade through the central district built across two large islands in the river Pregel, connected by seven bridges. The challenge was to devise a route that crossed every bridge once and once only. Euler proved that no such route existed.

Bristol, Thilo realised at the time, had 42 bridges connecting the various mainlands and islands formed by the River Avon and the Floating Harbour. By studying the layout, he was able to prove mathematically that a route which crosses each bridge once and once only is indeed possible. Moreover, he devised such a path and set out to walk it one February Saturday. Unfortunately, the journey, including both the Avonmouth Bridge to the West and the bridge near Hanham on the Eastern ringroad, stretched over 30 miles and took him from pre–dawn until well into the evening.

Thilo wrote about his walk in the Bristol Evening Post, and in a publication 50 Visions of Mathematics that I helped to edit for the 50th anniversary of the UK's Institute of Mathematics and its applications. The rest is history. Thilo met Jeff Lucas and the idea for this book was born. Forty-two bridges became 43, and now 45. Yet, Thilo tells me it is still possible to compose a walking route that crosses all of them once and once only — not that I recommend attempting it in a single day. Nevertheless, I hope readers who are inspired to visit the landmarks featured here will not just ponder on the history of Bristol, but will also use the time to think about networks, mathematics and the interconnectedness of everything.

Professor Alan Champneys, **Head of the Department of Engineering Mathematics, University of Bristol**

		Distance from start	Distance from previous bridge
1	Bristol Bridge	0km	
2	St Philip's Bridge	0.4km	400m
3	Castle Ditch Bridge	0.6km	200m
4	Temple Bridge	1.0km	400m
5	Valentine's Bridge	1.3km	300m
6	Meads Reach Bridge	1.5km	200m
7	Bath Bridge (West)	2.2km	700m
8	Bath Bridge (East)	2.4km	200m
9	Brock's Bridge	2.8km	400m
10	St Philip's Footbridge	3.0km	200m
11	Temple Meads Relief Line Bridge	3.2km	200m
12	Sparke Evans Park Bridge	4.7km	1.5km
13	St Philips Causeway Bridge (East)	5.0km	300m
14	St Philips Causeway Bridge (West)	5.4km	400m
15	Barton Hill Bridge	6.6km	1.2km
16	Netham Lock Bridge (East)	7.1km	500m
17	New Brislington Bridge	7.2km	100m
18	St Anne's Footbridge	7.8km	600m
19	Netham Lock Bridge (West)	8.4km	600m
20	Feeder Road Footbridge	9.4km	1km
21	Marsh Bridge	10.1km	700m
22	Totterdown Bridge	10.9km	800m
23	Langton St Bridge (Banana Bridge)	12.4km	1.5km
24	Bedminster Bridge (East)	12.8km	400m
25	Bedminster Bridge (West)	12.9km	100m
26	Bathurst Basin Footbridge	13.3km	400m
27	Bathurst Basin Roadbridge (East)	13.5km	200m
28	Bathurst Basin Roadbridge (West)	13.6km	100m
29	Gaol Ferry Bridge	13.9km	300m
30	Vauxhall Bridge	14.8km	900m
31	Ashton Avenue Bridge	15.5km	700m
32	Avon Bridge	15.8km	300m
33	South Entrance Lock Bridge	16.0km	200m
34	South Entrance Lock Walkway	16.2km	200m
35	Plimsoll Bridge	16.3km	100m
36	Clifton Suspension Bridge	17.3km	1km
37	Avonmouth Road Bridge	27.1km	9.8km
38	Portway Viaduct	34.1km	7km
39	Poole's Wharf Bridge	40.8km	6.7km
40	North Junction Lock Bridge	40.9km	100m
41	South Junction Lock Bridge	41.0km	100m
42	Prince Street Bridge	43.0km	2km
43	Pero's Bridge	43.2km	200m
44	Redcliffe Bridge	44.0km	800m
45	Castle Bridge	44.9km	900m
1	Bristol Bridge	45.2km	300m

© Open Street Map

8 | MAP

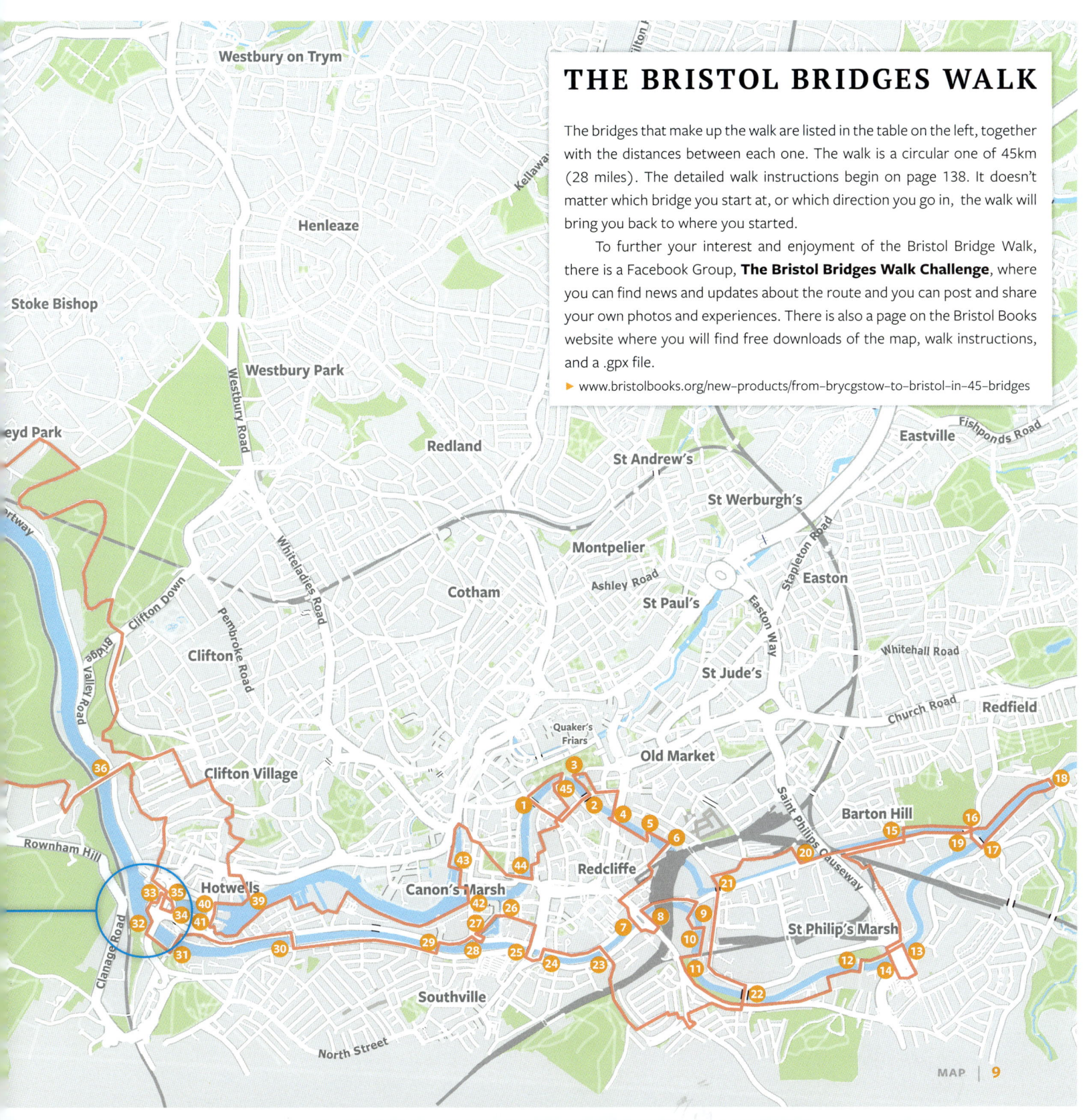

10 | BRISTOL BRIDGE

BRISTOL BRIDGE

Bristol began right here in the Saxon period, probably around the year 900. The Anglo–Saxon Chronicle of 1051 has the first written reference to Brycgstow (subsequent spellings vary), which means "place by the bridge". At first, the bridge may have been something like a set of floating pontoons which only later became a fixed timber bridge. As you stand on the modern bridge, look back towards Castle Green and try to imagine away the traffic and the buildings. Picture muddy banks with longboats resting on them, smoke rising from a cluster of huts, with trees in the distance. Imagine the silence!

This site ticked all the boxes for a fortified settlement which would protect against Viking raids — a rocky elevated spot surrounded by marshy flat plain almost encircled by two rivers, the Avon and the Frome. The settlement thrived on trade with Devon, Somerset, Wales and Ireland. By the mid–1100s, an early history book records that here was "almost the richest of all the towns in the Kingdom". By 1300, it was an international port and commercial centre with an impressive royal castle.

In the mid–13th century the timber bridge was replaced by something far more impressive — five pointed arches of Courtfield Stone from Monmouthshire about six metres wide. There were shops and houses up to five storeys high built on it each side of the roadway, perhaps modelled on London Bridge which had been built just 40 years earlier. In 1360, a chapel to Virgin Mary was added, built across an archway over the centre of the bridge, extending beyond it on flanking piers. At street level was a room used by the city council for meetings. On the next floor the chapel, surmounted by a bell

BRISTOL BRIDGE | 11

tower, straddled the bridge. The chapel was a grand space measuring 23m x 6.5m, and having four large windows on each side. A number of notable men were born in the houses on the bridge, such as William Thomas (born 1546), who became Archbishop of York.

By 1750, the bridge was 500-years-old and, according to Alexander Pope, crammed *"...with a strange mixture of seamen, women, children, loaded horses, asses and sledges with goods, dragging along altogether"*. But it was no longer fit for purpose. Carts often tipped over and *"many limbs and lives...(were)... lost by the narrow passage of Bristol Bridge."* Daniel Defoe's editor compared its narrowness with the minds of Bristolians. Something had to be done. After many years of argument about what a new bridge should look like, a three-arch design by the appropriately named James Bridges was chosen. The old bridge was demolished and the new one built on the same spot, using the existing mediaeval foundations. It was completed in 1768. The construction costs were a modest £10,300, but the necessary land purchases, demolition work, and numerous reports and surveys brought the total cost for the city corporation to £49,000 (roughly £10.5m at current value). It had imposing Portland Stone balustrades and four small stone toll booths, one at each corner. No more houses on the bridge — that was old-fashioned.

In 1793, Bristol Bridge gained notoriety as the scene of a horrific massacre of civilians by the military. On Sept 29th of that year, having paid to cross the bridge for 25 years, Bristolians widely expected that all tolls would be abolished. And indeed they were, to great euphoria and celebration. However, the Bridge Commissioners had got their sums wrong, and promptly tried to reinstate some of the tolls nine days later. A public disturbance, which began with the burning down of the bridge's wooden gates, escalated over the next two days. Eventually an angry crowd gathered several thousand strong. A replacement set of gates was set on fire. The Riot Act was read. The militia who had assembled on the bridge fired 100 rounds of live ammunition into the crowd, killing 11 and wounding 45. It soon became clear that many of these were innocent bystanders. But despite huge public pressure no official enquiry was ever held into one of the worst civilian massacres of the 18th century. No one was brought to trial or even held to account.

Sadly, the present appearance of the bridge bears no relation to its former glories. It was widened in 1861 (east side) and again in 1873 (west side) by placing cast iron "wings" each side, supported by additional columns which obscure much of the original stonework. Even then this aesthetic degeneration caused controversy. At the same time, the stone toll booths were demolished and the stone balustrades replaced with ones of cast iron. In the 1960s, the wrecking job was completed when the latter were replaced with the present dull railings. We must now be content with recalling the past splendours of Bristol Bridge rather than contemplating it's current state.

ST PHILIP'S BRIDGE

St Philip's Bridge, like Bristol Bridge, is located in the heart of mediaeval Bristol. A ferry crossing was established here in the 12th century, linking Old Market with the Temple area. In 1651, the Corporation took it over from the private operator, calling it the Bathavon ferry. The name changed over the centuries to Queen Street ferry, then Temple Back ferry, then Counterslip ferry – the latter name derived from the "Countess Slip" on the south bank. From the early 19th to well into the 20th century, the area immediately upstream of the bridge was the centre of the manufacturing city, dominated by heavy industry such as iron foundries, lead works, gas works, glass making and soap manufacture. The ferry became a very busy crossing point and there was clearly a case for a bridge. In 1837, a company was set up to build one, financed by private capital from local influential citizens. Firstly, it bought the ferry from the Corporation for £2,157. This was carrying an estimated 300 passengers per day, a considerable number considering the then small size of the city (In 1801, only 64,000 inhabitants). A temporary wooden bridge was constructed in 1838 and removed when the new bridge was finished. The new bridge was a grand thing, *"handsome, elegant and airy"* with a two-arched span of Pennant Sandstone, with a central drawbridge. It was designed in Gothic and Tudor style by a Mr. Gravatt, an engineer. It cost £11,000.

The Bristol railway companies had taken a keen interest in how the bridge was to be designed. They applied considerable pressure to the Bridge Company to ensure that the new bridge was one which opened and would not therefore impede river traffic of any height — because this traffic was carrying goods that could be or had been transported by rail. The railway companies eventually contributed more than a third of the cost of the bridge in order to get their way. Evidence suggests that the railway directors were also expecting to get the (fixed) Bristol Bridge modified to be an opening bridge as well.

The bridge was opened in December 1841 by the Lord Mayor with considerable razzamatazz including a procession of the city's dignitaries through the streets. Three hearty cheers were taken up *"by the vast crowd assembled"* and this was accompanied by the firing of cannon and ringing of churchbells. A banquet then ensued for all the VIP's. During the first 12 months, nearly 1,000 people a day were crossing it for a toll of half a penny. Although it was acknowledged that the company was not charging the full market rate to cross the bridge, over the next 30 years annoyance grew at

14 | ST PHILIP'S BRIDGE

having to pay the toll. The Corporation, bowing to pressure, took over the bridge in 1874 and made it toll-free in 1875 which *"occasioned considerable rejoicing amongst those more particularly benefited"*. St Philips bridge was known as the "Ha'penny Bridge" long after its toll had been abolished.

In 1876-77, it was widened and strengthened. The drawbridge part was removed and made fixed; it seems that the feared restrictions this might have on river traffic movement had not materialised. For the next 70 years, St Philip's bridge faded unnoticed into the background of city life. But on 11th April 1941, just nine months short of its 100th birthday, it became the only bridge in Bristol to be hit by a German bomb in the Second World War. Bristol and Avonmouth suffered 29 bombing raids from November 1940 to July 1941, nine of them major. The targets were primarily the docks, Temple Meads Railway Station and nearby goods yards. The bombing inaccuracy of the time meant that much civilian damage was caused. It is estimated that 10,000 high explosive and 100,000 incendiary bombs were dropped on the city during the war. A total of 1,159 people were killed and as many seriously injured, 46,000 houses were damaged and 2,500 were completely destroyed. Forty acres of the of the central area were reduced to rubble. Many historic buildings were lost. Streets entirely or partly destroyed in the centre included Broadmead, Thomas Street, Victoria Street, Park Street, Queens Road and Redcliffe Street. Castle Park, which you can see downstream from here, is now an open green space, but until the bombs fell it used to be one of the most densely built and busiest areas of the city.

St Philip's bridge took a direct hit on its western arch. This severed the power cables for the tramway system, all of which was carried by the bridge. The arch was immediately rebuilt in utility manner to get the city moving again but the tramways, already on the point of obsolescence, were replaced by buses and never came back into service. The repaired bridge was replaced by the utterly characterless present one in 1967-8. A small remnant of the stonework of the original bridge can be seen set into the end wall of a terraced row above the steps leading down to the water on the north bank. A miniature tower stands on a column to give us a hint of what we have lost.

The cityscape here is dominated by the magnificent former Tramways Electricity Generating Station right next to the bridge on the south bank. A hybrid of Neoclassical and Baroque styles, this is one of Bristol's best buildings, designed in 1899 by the London architect William Curtis Green at the very start of a distinguished career (he was probably keen to make a good impression!). As the name implies, it was the powerhouse for the whole of the pre-war electric tram system of Bristol. The other building worthy of note here is the tall grey concrete Shot Tower (1969) a little way upstream, which was used for making lead shot.

ST PHILIP'S BRIDGE | 15

16 | CASTLE DITCH BRIDGE

CASTLE DITCH BRIDGE

This bridge stands on the edge of Castle Park — Bristol's most historic location — the site of Bristol Castle and its Watergate, both long since demolished.

The western end of the area we now call Castle Park was first occupied by the Saxons. They probably built some kind of timber stockade on this defensible area of higher ground. After the Norman conquest (1066), William the Conqueror gave the manor of Barton Regis, which included Bristol, to his half-brother Geoffrey Mowbray, Bishop of Coutances, who built a timber "motte and bailey" slightly north of the centre of the park. Thirty or 40 years later, around 1110, the third owner, Robert Fitzroy, Earl of Gloucester, rebuilt it in a more substantial manner in stone, extended the outer curtain wall and gave the city one of the strongest and most impressive fortresses in England. The keep was huge, about 30m square and 33m high. The walls were 8m thick at the base. Only the keeps at the Tower of London and Colchester were bigger. It had four massive towers at each corner and possibly a fifth. The outer curtain walls eventually enclosed precincts of about 4.5 ha.

Henry II (1133–1189) confiscated the castle from the Earl of Gloucester's son, William, when the latter supported a rebellion against the King. Henry spent some of his childhood in the castle and as an adult he stationed his troops here. Bristol Castle had become a Royal Castle — the third largest in the country. Henry III and his successor, Edward I, improved it further. A chronicler wrote *"the town was almost the richest in*

CASTLE DITCH BRIDGE | 17

the country owing to its foreign and domestic trade, while its castle, standing on a mighty mound, was garrisoned by crowds of knights and soldiers". The castle housed some significant prisoners. The two sons of the last free ruler of Wales, when aged less than five, were imprisoned here in 1283 for the rest of their lives. Henry III held his granddaughter, Princess Eleanor of Brittany, who had a good claim to the throne, captive for 40 years "under gentle house arrest". At least 17 of those years, possibly all (accounts vary), were spent in Bristol Castle until she died in 1241.

The present bridge stands at the junction of Castle Ditch with the River Avon. This short stretch of water leading off the Floating Harbour, which now comes to a halt after some 30m or so at Queen Street, is the last visible "echo" of the castle moat.

The moat passed through a "watergate" in the outer wall to allow ships to enter the castle's precincts to load/unload. The Watergate of Bristol Castle is the centrepiece of the city's mediaeval Coat of Arms. It is depicted with two huge drum towers that create an imposing and forbidding edifice — a symbol of the city's strength and potency. Archaeological excavations have uncovered a probable (but not conclusive) structure for the watergate about 50m northwest of the modern bridge, where Castle Street turns to the right at its north end. It seems likely that the Castle Ditch we see now cuts through a wide "shelf" of man-made ground subsequently constructed in front of the castle's outer wall and may not be the line of the original moat. Conjectural illustrations of the Watergate, and drawings that place it at the site of the modern bridge, which appear in some older Bristol history books, are not based on evidence and should be regarded as fanciful.

After the War of the Roses, the castle fell into disuse and

ruin. In 1652, Oliver Cromwell ordered it to be demolished. The area previously enclosed by the castle walls rapidly became one of the most densely built-over parts of the city and it remained so until German bombing in 1940 flattened a great deal of it. Many of the buildings that were lost were hundreds of years old.

Very little of the castle and its outbuildings are left — you need to look hard to find the remains. A part of one of the outbuildings, dating from around 1225, still stands in the park, called the Castle Chambers.

The rather neglected Castle Ditch fake drawbridge which you cross is late-20th century and may be the first to span the moat since the 17th century. Alas, it is a poor thing of which there is little to say except that in no way does it do justice to its historic location. Bristol City Council ought to prioritise its replacement with something of quality that is far more thoughtful.

TEMPLE BRIDGE

This bridge, together with the contemporaneous Redcliffe Bridge, were the first bridges in Bristol to be built for the purpose of relieving motor vehicle traffic congestion, rather than, for example, shortening journey distances, replacing a ferry, or giving better access to new parts of the expanding city.

Even before the First World War, Bristol Bridge had become a notorious bottleneck for motor traffic. The congestion spread in the first decades of the 20th century to include Baldwin Street, Redcliffe Street and Victoria Street. At that time these streets were Bristol's primary shopping areas and the focal point of the city. The problem was that many of the central streets, still basically mediaeval, were narrow and all tended to converge on Bristol Bridge. Bristol City Council convened a special committee in 1928 to consider the problem and, as a result of this and subsequent deliberations during the 1930s, it was decided that the city needed a new eastern route and a new western route around the central area. Work began on these schemes in the late 1930s. These radical interventions were to change the face of the city and leave a lasting legacy just as much as the construction of the New Cut had done some 140 years before, and as much as German bombing in World War Two was to do in the decade ahead.

Temple Bridge was part of the new "Eastern Road", now called Redcliffe Way and Temple Way, intended to speed traffic between the south end of Victoria Street and Old Market. The bridge completed the road scheme in April 1939, at a time when there was growing concern about a coming war and precautions for air raids. It was made, like many others in Bristol, by the Bristol engineering firm of John Lysaght. It has seven parallel steel joists braced together. It was built in three sections; the middle part was floated in on a barge and joined to the other sections that had been built out from the banks. It is a fixed bridge — there are no moving

parts. The bridge itself cost around £22,000, about a tenth of the total cost of the road scheme.

It took the Planning and Public Works Committee a couple of years to get round to deciding on names for the new roads. The initial idea was for "Temple Highway" and "Redcliffe Highway" but the members of the committee thought "Highway" was too redolent of Dick Turpin and robbery, so they decided to drop the "high".

For many years, a wide dual carriageway from Old Market was squeezed onto the narrow bridge. In 1970s the bridge was doubled in width by adding a new section on the west side and the whole road widened to Temple Gate. The abutments were refaced with quality brickwork in an attractive postmodern, vaguely Byzantine, style which matches the vaguely Byzantine postmodern brickwork of the nearby buildings. The lamps which sit atop the brick pillars may look antique, but in fact are good modern "repro". Those who appreciate the aesthetics of rivetting will enjoy the underside of the older half of the bridge. Rivetting only gave way to the welding of steelwork in the 1950s and early 60s.

VALENTINE'S BRIDGE

Valentine's Bridge opened in the year 2000. It cost £500,000, paid for by private finance as a condition for the granting of planning permission for office development. Looking north from the south bank, it forms an impressive pairing with the silvery fin–like tower of "The Eye" office block behind it, each echoing the curves of the other. Although it looks as if the bridge was designed with the tower in mind, it preceded it by nine years.

Atkins Structures won a limited competition for the design of this 48 m span footbridge. The main contractor was Alfred McAlpine Civil Engineering Ltd. The fabrication and assembly was done offsite by specialist fabricator S H

Structures of North Yorkshire, and the bridge was craned in as a single piece weighing around 50 tonnes. The deck is supported by cables radiating from a single 25m high inclined mast. The curves of the deck are defined by a 60cm diameter tubular spine, part of a truss that is triangular in cross-section. Make a point of having a look at the bridge from the underneath, its backbone resembles a creature from an science fiction movie!

None of the buildings you see around here are more than 20-years-old except for Temple Meads station immediately to the south. Valentines Bridge, and the next bridge on the walk, Meads Reach Bridge are in the heart of, and owe their existence to, the Temple Quarter Enterprise Zone. This is a "mixed use" development which started life as "Quay Point", initiated by the now defunct Bristol Development Corporation in 1989. Since then it has expanded to cover a total of 100 hectares and is now one of the largest regeneration projects in the UK. It will include a new £300m campus for Bristol University. The aim is to attract 22,000 jobs here over the next 25 years. Several government departments have their regional base here including the Homes and Communities Agency, The Planning Inspectorate, Ofsted, and English Heritage.

The area of the south bank between this bridge and Meads Reach Bridge which you see a little way upstream, remained pastureland (that is to say, "*meades*") until the mid-1800s when Temple Meads station, a huge railway goods shed, and the short-lived "Brunels" dock were built. The latter was only demolished in the 1980s. On the north bank stood The Phoenix Glassworks from the late 18th century until it closed in 1923, from which Glass Wharf takes its name. It had three huge brick kilns. The "Eye" towerblock stands pretty much on the exact site of the eastern kiln.

The clunky building on the south bank that overlooks Valentine's Bridge is not the local branch of Dartmoor Prison but the former Bristol and West Building Society, completed in 2000. This stands on the site of the former fortified Harraz Tower, part of Bristol's 13th-century city wall (called "The Portwall"), which continued from here to the west along what is now Rivergate and is commemorated there by "Six Portwall Markers", a sculpture consisting of six black granite blocks.

MEADS REACH BRIDGE

Meads Reach Bridge, opened in 1998 and soon nicknamed "the Cheesegrater", is Bristol's finest example of *the bridge as sculpture*. In 2010, it was given an award by the Institution of Structural Engineers. The Judges thought it "*...both an outstanding work of art and a highly innovative structure*".

If its smooth sleek minimalist lines put you vaguely in mind of a stealth bomber, maybe it's because it was designed and built with 3D–modelling computer software used to design aircraft wings. It is a "stressed skin" single box of stainless steel. As the term implies, the whole surface (except for the deck) is as much a part of the structure under stress loading as is the internal stiffening. The geometry is complex, with variation in depth, curvature in elevation, and variation in width across the span.

This competition-winning design was intended as a fusion of three disciplines: architecture, civil engineering and, unusually, the art of lighting. An important design intention was that the bridge should not be lit but should *be the light*. It has to been seen at dusk or night-time to appreciate this, when the internal lighting streams out from the 55,000 holes in the steel skin, creating a truly magical experience. The holes vary in size and are larger (40mm max) where the stresses in the bridge are lower and smaller (10 mm min) where the stresses are larger. In effect, they become a visual expression of the stress distribution in the bridge and hence the need for highly sophisticated computer modelling. As is usual with the "less-is-more" school of design, a great deal of complicated effort is needed to make something look plain and simple. When the result is a thing of beauty, as here, the effort (and cost) can be worth it. The cost was, in fact, an eye-watering £2.4m, but as with Valentine's Bridge, this was not borne by the public purse. The bridge was financed privately as a condition of planning consent for nearby development.

It is constructed from top quality 6mm 2205 duplex stainless steel. The perforations were cut by computer-controlled lasers. The steel plates were preformed and invisibly welded end-to-end to form eight sections each up to 7m long. These were transported to the site and fully assembled on the riverbank into a single 75 tonne structure, before it was finally craned into position. Accolades for this beautiful object are due to architects Niall McLaughlin, structural engineers Price and Myers, and lighting artist Martin Richman. It was fabricated by M-tec of Darwen in Lancashire.

The bridge has not been without its troubles, however. It is part of the Sustrans National Cycling Network and was designed with this in mind. During installation the specification of the decking was changed without the approval

of the architects. Owing to a spate of cycling accidents in wet conditions, due to its slippery surface, 600 cyclists signed a petition which resulted in the bridge being resurfaced in 2014. In 2017, a contractor's lorry was driven over this pedestrian-only bridge resulting in substantial damage. It was closed for over a year.

It is interesting to compare this footbridge stylistically to Valentine's Bridge of two years earlier, just a few metres away along the quayside. The two design philosophies could not be more different. Meads Reach is rationalist, minimalist, super-cool, less-is-more. Valentine's is postmodern retro, showy, full of curvy movement. Neo-Baroque you might say. Which one do you prefer?

BATH BRIDGES (East and West)

The current (East) Bath Bridge dates from 1909–10 but has two antecedents. You may not wish to linger on it — the two previous bridges both collapsed in the space of 50 years!

When the course of the River Avon was diverted into the "New Cut" in 1809, the plan devised by William Jessop provided for two identical new bridges over it to be built — one here where the eastern bridge now stands, called "Hill's Bridge", and another at Bedminster called "Harford's Bridge". These were the first bridges in Bristol to span the River Avon since Bristol Bridge nearly 1,000 years earlier. Two members of the Hill family were directors of the Port Authority which commissioned them, Charles and Thomas, and it is unclear which particular Hill the bridge was named after — perhaps both of them!

Both bridges were made of cast iron, designed by Jessop and made by the famous Coalbrookdale Company of Ironbridge Gorge in Shropshire. The use of this material in bridge construction at that time was still novel. This is evidenced by the fact that, in 1806, two years after construction began and on the point of completion, Hill's Bridge completely collapsed, probably due to a fault in the design of the ironwork. Five people were injured and two died. Construction had to begin again and eventually the bridge was opened in 1809. Like their famous cousin at Coalbrookdale, Hill's and Harford's bridges were light and elegant, with a single arch comprised of a series of six slender curved ribs of cast iron, parallel with each other 2m apart, resting on stone abutments. The arched ribs supported vertical cast iron pillars that supported the road deck. The two bridges were sufficiently cutting edge to warrant an inclusion as a case study in Charles Hutton's monograph *"Tracts on Mathematical and Philosophical Subjects"* in 1812.

In 1820, Hill's Bridge suffered some damage when it was hit by a coal barge and two supporting ribs were damaged. Thirty-five years later, on the morning of 20th March 1855, one year short of its 50th anniversary, this unfortunate bridge met its nemesis in the form of *"John"*, a 180-ton steam barge heading downstream towards the bridge. The tide in the New Cut was ebbing faster than usual. The barge went out of control and hit the bridge structure on the north side with so much force that, despite the flow of water against it, the barge rebounded several metres. With an enormous crash the whole of the bridge immediately disappeared into the water, taking up to 20 people with it. Most managed to survive but there were between two and five fatalilties (reports vary). The barge carried on to Bedminster Bridge and very nearly hit that. At BathustBasin, a constable who

had been following its progress took the master into custody. He was later prosecuted for negligence. All bridge traffic was immediately diverted to Harford's (Bedminster) Bridge. As the latter was of identical design, the city authorities rapidly had it surveyed and strengthened. The disaster was reported in detail in the local press but was also considered significant enough to warrant an article in the Illustrated London News, accompanied by an engraving of the scene after the collapse.

A new bridge was put in hand within a month — an indication of how important this crossing was for the commerce of the city (in 1880 we know it carried 1,786 vehicles and 9,000 pedestrians in a day). It was designed and constructed by Edward Finch and Co of Chepstow. It consisted of nine parallel girders spanning the river, each 32m long and about 25 tonnes in weight, brought to this site from Chepstow by barge and steamer.

In the Victorian era the Leander Swimming Club used to stage an annual swimming race along the New Cut from Bath Bridge downstream to the former Rownham Ferry, near Cumberland Basin. But eventually, owing to the ever increasing industrial pollution of the water, they were forced to abandon the event in the 1880s.

The cast-iron 1855 bridge was replaced in its turn, in 1909–10, by the wider, steel eastern one we see now. The balustrades replicate the previous ones. The name Hill's Bridge fell into disuse. Bath Bridge, as it is now known, is today part of a busy traffic junction hostile to pedestrians and so largely goes unheeded, which is a pity, as it is certainly worth a few minutes of your time. The deck is slightly curved and this, together with the vertebrae-like supports for the balustrade, make it look like the arched backbone of some strange riparian. The barley-sugar twisted balustrade railings are lovely and there is a very finely detailed coat-of-arms in the centre of the balustrade. Bath Bridge was "doubled" with a dull western bridge in 1959 to relieve traffic congestion.

BROCK'S BRIDGE

This bridge, completed in 2016, was initially intended to be a key route to the site of a 12,000 seat Bristol Arena which was to have been built on "Arena Island", a large brownfield site next to Temple Meads station previously used as a railway maintenance depot. The site is bounded by the railway lines entering Temple Meads, Bath Road and the New Cut. This area is a part of the Temple Quarter Enterprise Zone — a huge regeneration scheme with Temple Meads station roughly at its geographical centre. The bridge cost £11m and was funded by the Government's Homes and Communities Agency. The plan initiated by the then–mayor George Ferguson, in 2014 was to build an arena here, but this was cancelled in 2018 by his successor, Marvin Rees, and the arena is now destined for the suburbs. But the bridge remains and has the distinction of being the first new road bridge across the Avon for 100 years. The site, renamed Temple Island, will now be given over to a conference centre, hotel, housing and commercial space.

Brock's Bridge is 63m long and 18m wide. Pedestrians and cycles are segregated from vehicles. The total weight of steel

is 820 tonnes. The bridge superstructure was designed by Pell Frischmann, an international structural and civil engineering firm. It was fabricated in Italy as a 137-piece "kit of parts" by the Italian Cimolai Group, a huge conglomerate of civil engineering and construction companies which also made the steelwork for the Second Severn Crossing. The foundations and abutments were constructed by Dublin-based John Sisk and Son, another large firm operating internationally.

The bridge parts were brought to Bristol by 40ft lorries and assembled on the riverbank in four months by a team of 25 welders, with the long axis at right angles to the river. An ingenious method was used to get the bridge in place over the water. A light steel frame, the "nose", as long again as the bridge, was attached to the bridge on the end nearest the river. Concrete weights were placed on the landward end. Temporary steel pads were fitted on the underside of the bridge which allowed it to move forwards on sets of rollers. It was then possible to project the "bridge plus nose" assembly horizontally across the river with a winch and pulley system, just like sliding a ruler across a gap between two desks. As it slid across the gap between the banks, the concrete weights on the landward end prevented the unsupported end from tipping into the water. When the bridge was over the supports on the far bank, the concrete weights at the other end were removed, which allowed the leading end to settle onto the supports. The "nose" was then removed. The bridge had to be moved very slowly, with progress being constantly monitored and small adjustments being made. The operation took 20 hours, but had it not been interrupted by visiting dignitaries and council officials, it would have taken around 10 hours. There are 348m of concrete piles in the foundations.

Communications cables run underneath the bridge, together with piping for a district heating network which will distribute low carbon heat and power to the site from a local energy centre. The network is divided into different sections that cover areas across the city, and the first section to be completed will feed directly into the Temple Enterprise Zone, as well as parts of the city centre and Redcliffe.

In early 2016, the Bristol Post newspaper ran a competition to name the new bridge. The winning name, Brock's Bridge, was submitted by the Totterdown and Knowle Local History Society and commemorates local Victorian builder and entrepreneur William Brock (1830 – 1907).

Brock, the son of a shoemaker, was a self-taught craftsman and builder originally from Devon. He moved to Totterdown in the 1850s, and started a joinery and building business next to Temple Meads station which became very successful. After 20 years the business moved to a riverbank site on Albert Road in St Philip's Marsh (just 500m southwest of the bridge), close to where Totterdown Bridge would be built. He and his business partner, Robert Bruce, were now employing 250 people in their "Steam Joinery" where three steam engines powered a huge range of the latest joinery machinery — some designed by Brock himself — that could handle 20m long logs unloaded from ships berthed on the riverbank. In 1883, The Bristol Times and Mirror ran a long descriptive article about the Steam Joinery. In rhapsodic Brontean prose we are advised that *"no visitor to the steam joinery works can fail to remark to what an extraordinary pitch of perfection the machinery here in every branch has been brought"*.

As well as his joinery, Brock also had a sizeable building construction workforce and he was involved in the construction of St Philip's Bridge, Bedminster Bridge and the widening of Bristol Bridge. He built railway stations at Taunton and Weston-super-Mare, and his other projects included building the "Swiss House" in Leigh Woods, a landmark overlooking the Avon Gorge near the Clifton Suspension Bridge.

When Totterdown Bridge was built, the alterations needed to Albert Road effectively cut his premises in two, affecting his business. Although he had been an enthusiastic campaigner for the new bridge he became involved in

litigation against Bristol City Council for compensation which delayed the full opening of the bridge for over a year. Sadly, Brock and Bruce's business went bankrupt in 1894 for unknown reasons, but probably because there was a downturn in the type of work they had been involved in.

As for Brock's Bridge itself, in terms of aesthetics, it is regrettably stolid and dull. This is both surprising and disappointing, given its prominent location. It is an off-the-shelf bow bridge that has no relationship to its context and no attempt has been made to deal with the difference in levels between the riverbanks. Consequently, the slope of the bridge makes it look unstable and ill-at-ease.

ST PHILIP'S FOOTBRIDGE

This splendid footbridge is the sister to Brock's Bridge (chapter 9) and together they were part of the plan for public access to the Bristol Arena originally intended to be sited on Temple Island. This space will be filled by a conference centre, hotel, housing and commercial space. St Philip's Footbridge was designed by Knight Architects of High Wycombe and the consulting engineers were CH2M. The steel was fabricated by SH Structures of North Yorkshire and the installation was by Andrew Scott Ltd of Port Talbot. The cost was £3.1m, borne by the Government's Homes and Communities Agency. It was installed in 2018.

The solid but simple and slender shapes of the bridge are in high contrast to the two flanking bridges, Brock's Bridge and The Temple Meads Relief Line Bridge (chapter 11), with their airy, busy steelwork. On the west bank it sits next to the impressive giant brick arches of the Victorian retaining wall of the former railway depot. On the east bank it lands on the riverside path, which would be quite rural were it not for the adjacent industrial estate. It is Y-shaped in plan, 50m long, a generous 4m wide, and has two diverging landings at the east end — stairs and ramp. Cycle use requires the high handrail. The deck has a slight gradient from one end to the other. This avoids the need for an intermediate landing "break" and it means that as you walk onto the bridge from the west side, it feels as though the ground is extended naturally over the river, rather than "walking onto a bridge".

The main challenge for the designers was to make a bridge that would accommodate the 5m height difference between

the two sides of the river, the 10.5m clearance required above the average water level (to allow navigation by rivercraft) and the very limited landing space on the riverside path on the east bank. In addition, the designers wanted to avoid support piers in the water to minimise environmental impact. The riverbank population includes kingfishers, otters and bats!

The constricted landing space on the east side was solved by the Y-plan split landings, which also has the advantage that when eastbound users pause to choose their exit, they are not directly overlooking unsightly industrial back yards. This configuration also allowed the staircase and ramp on the lower bank to be smoothly integrated into the overall form of the bridge, rather than looking like bolt-on extras.

Because of space constraints on the lower bank, a gradient on the bridge deck could not be entirely eliminated. The designers therefore came up with a very ingenious way of hiding it. A smooth transition has been made from the west end of the bridge, where the deck is entirely supported by structural steelwork from underneath (as a tapering box girder), to the east end where the structural steelwork is above the deck (as a U-shaped channel in which the deck sits). This is given visual expression as a sloping line of parapet steelwork working in opposition to the slope of the walkway. This masks the slope of the deck and also brings a satisfying complexity to the side views of the bridge.

There are three abutments (foundations) in view of the Y-shaped plan. Each is of reinforced concrete resting on piles 15–20m deep. There is a 60m long concrete access ramp on the east bank. A great deal of design effort went into making this as minimalist as possible. The result is attractive and understated. The top slab seems to be an extension of the bridge, while its main bulk and a large sensually shaped corbel appear to emerge from the ground to support it from below.

The bridge handrail comprises simple vertical plates. When you see these from the side, they disappear and give the form of the bridge a very crisp profile, but in skewed views, the plates seem to overlap and feel "protecting". LED lighting runs along the handrail as a continuous blade of light.

As well as taking account of the design constraints already referred to, the designers also had to make sure the bridge was light enough to be prefabricated and lifted into place by a crane. Which it was.

St Philip's Footbridge is a brilliant example of how aesthetic, structural and functional needs have been simultaneously met by thoughtful and painstaking design to create one of Bristol's most beautiful bridges. To a setting which is rather a mish-mash, it brings a quiet, still point of modernist order. Ten out of ten.

TEMPLE MEADS RELIEF LINE BRIDGE

Also known as the Great Western Relief Line Bridge, the Bristol Relief Line Bridge, the Temple Meads Avoiding Line Bridge, and the St Philip's Marsh Avoiding Line Bridge.

This steel railway–plus–footbridge dates from 1892 and is a bridge of three spans, 210m long in total. The section over the water which incorporates the footbridge is one of Bristol's most delightful bridges. The two sections that carry the railway over Victor Street and Albert Road are for track only.

A symphony of rhythmic lines and curves rests on

massive round black pillars that look like upended boilers from ancient steam trains. The repainting of the steelwork in bright "Bristol Blue" is a probably unintended masterstroke that makes it even livelier.

The bridge was built for Great Western Railway Company by Henry Lovatt of Wolverhampton for £6,000. On the Totterdown side a sizeable new cutting was simultaneously excavated to take the railway line through Pylle Hill, adjacent to Victoria Park. A temporary wooden bridge was constructed over the river to take wagons of excavated earth away to St Philip's Marsh — the new railway bridge was constructed over the top of it and then the temporary structure was dismantled.

All the rivetting in the bridge was done by hand. The sinking of the 2.4m diameter cylindrical pillars which had to go more than 4.6m into the watery ground was acheived by working inside them in compressed air. An initial segment of pillar was weighted to force it into the ground as far as possible. An airlock was fitted to the top and the pressure inside raised to 2.8 bars. This kept water out of the pillar segment and workmen entered by the airlock to dig out and remove soil and rock. As this was removed, the pillar segment sank further. The airlock was removed, a new segment fitted on top and the airlock placed on top of that. Segments of pillar were added and sunk until the required depth was reached. The space inside was then filled with concrete. Working in compressed air is now a highly regulated and controlled practice in view of the risks to health from decompression sickness (otherwise known as "the bends"). But in the late 19th century there were no such regulations and the precautions needed to avoid the risks were poorly understood. History does not record whether any workmen were seriously affected.

The nearby Totterdown Bridge had opened a few years before. This provided the inhabitants of Totterdown with just a short walk or ride to St Philip's Marsh, where many of them worked but its location had been much debated and for many it was too far upstream. The construction of the relief line bridge was an opportunity to relieve this problem. The additional cost of incorporating a footbridge into it was paid for by Bristol City Council – a much cheaper solution than building a separate footbridge. Result – happiness!

The purpose of the relief line and bridge was initially to enable goods trains to bypass Temple Meads station but soon non–stop passenger trains from London to the southwest also used it. When the St Philip's Marsh locomotive maintenance depot was opened in 1906 it also became the route into the depot. Nowadays, the line is normally only used for this latter purpose although still classified as a main line. For decades the depot was used for maintenence of InterCity High Speed Trains, but now that these have almost been phased out, only Diesel Multiple Units (DMU's) remain to be serviced there by a workforce of about 240.

SPARKE EVANS PARK BRIDGE

Question: what does Sparke Evans Park have in common with the Torres del Paine National Park in Patagonia? Answer: a bridge like this one, designed by the same company!

Sparke Evans Park Bridge is one of the highlights of the Bristol bridge walk. It is a light, elegant, steel suspension footbridge with steel basketwork balustrades. It is similar to Gaol Ferry bridge in Southville, designed a year earlier by the same firm — David Rowell and Co. of London. As a plaque proclaims, it was built by the local engineering firm of John

Lysaght in 1933. The bridge was built as a part of Bristol City Council's many job creation schemes of the 1920s and 30s to relieve unemployment. Brislington Bridge was another such project (chapter 17).

Rowell's company began life in 1855 as a fencing business but then diversified into iron frame buildings and then small elegant suspension bridges between 1903 and 1951. The company was liquidated in 1970 but quite a few of their bridges still exist. Most of them are in Britain but there is one in the Falkland Islands, one in New Zealand and, after visiting Sparke Evans Park, if you ever find yourself driving through the Torres del Paine National Park in Patagonia, and crossing the "Black Bridge", you will have a strange feeling of Bristolian deja vu.

Although in not quite as dramatic a location as the Patagonian National Park, it is the setting here next to the park that, in summer and autumn, makes it a five-star delight with it's backdrop of trees on both sides of the river and the adjacent park on the north side. You might spot tufted ducks, mallards, coots and moorhens on the riverbanks.

Sparke Evans Park is a roughly rectangular tree-lined green oasis of seven acres. It was a mainly residential area when the land was presented to the City Corporation in 1902 on condition that it was to be used as public pleasure grounds. The donor was a group of philanthropists headed by Peter Fabyan Sparke Evans (1826–1905), a partner in the nearby Avonside Tannery (on Feeder Road near Barton Hill Bridge, but long gone). Sparke Evans was a shrewd businessman but also a significant Bristol philanthropist. His family came from South Devon. He was taught the tanning business by his father. In the 1860s, with his father and brothers, he established a tannery here at St Philip's Marsh, and also at Wapping Wharf, and another in Bedminster. Evans was a nonconformist and was Deacon of Highbury Congregational Church, Cotham, and Member of the "Committee for Promoting the Better Housing of the Poor". His obituary in the Western Daily Press said he was *"a gentleman who in a quiet way was given to many good works"*.

The park contains a rose garden which, in its heyday, had a high reputation, diseases being allegedly kept at bay due to soot and fumes from the coal fired trains in the nearby St Philip's Marsh railway depot. On the far west edge of the park, and worth a short detour, are the dilapidated remains of a shelter dating from 1925 with attractive wrought-iron pillars and decorative brackets. The Avon Walkway runs along the southern edge of the park.

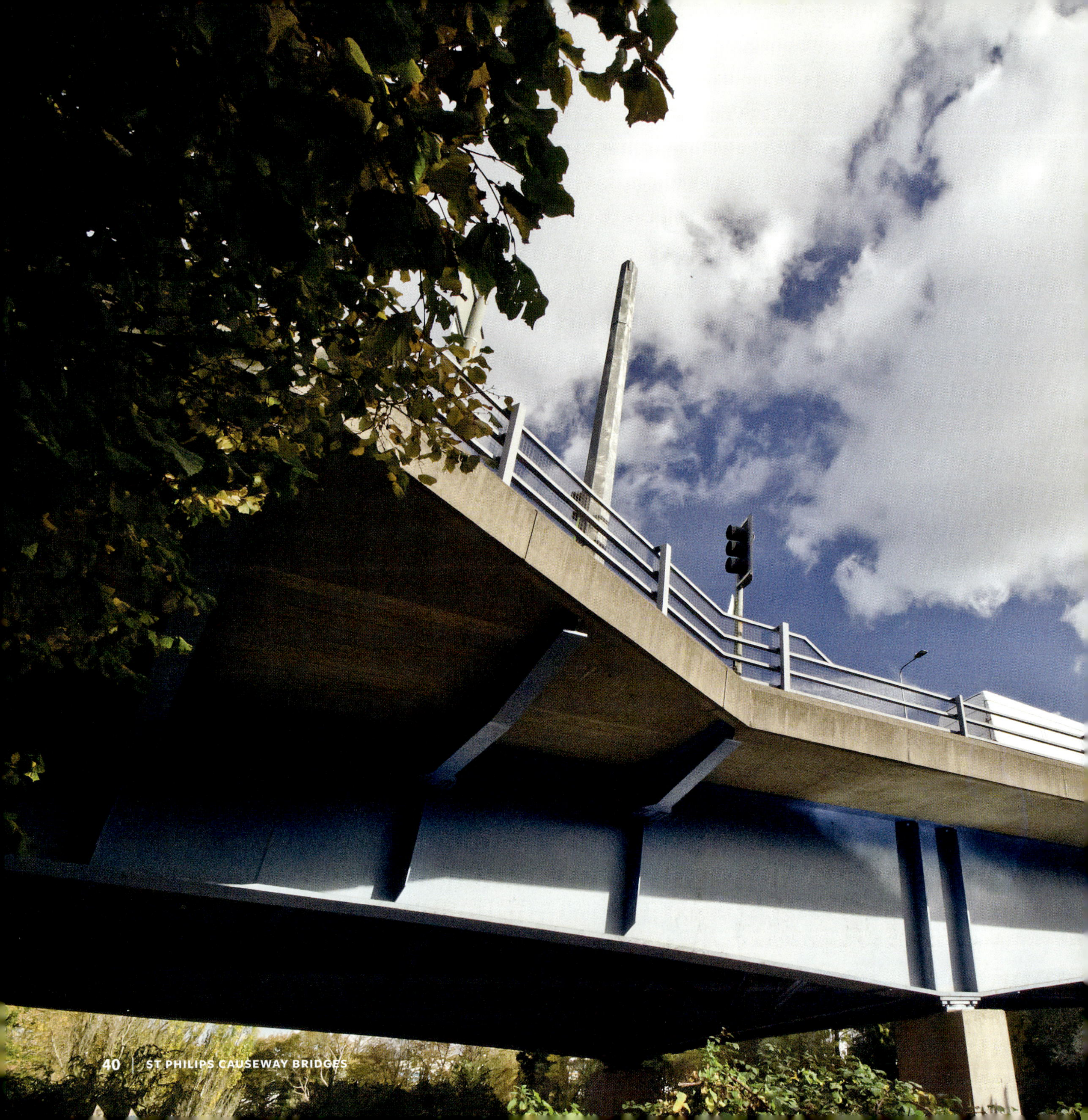

ST PHILIPS CAUSEWAY BRIDGES

(East and West)

13 14

St Philips Causeway is an urban dual carriageway linking the M4 and M32 with the Bristol–Bath section of the A4. It was originally known as the "Spine Road" and was renamed after a public competition. It is 2.2km long, incorporating this pair of bridges and another pair over the Feeder Canal. The whole scheme took two years to complete, cost £55m and was opened in July 1994. This road, together with a proposed weir (never realised) on the River Avon near Bathurst Basin, were the main projects of a masterplan created by the Bristol Development Corporation (BDC). The BDC was created by the government with an initial budget of £15m (later increased to fund the road) to regenerate a huge 365ha area east of the city centre which took in Temple Meads, St Philip's Marsh, some of Totterdown, the length of the Feeder, St Anne's and Crew's Hole. The size of the area involved was eventually somewhat reduced. The main contractor for the road and bridges was Balfour Beatty, and Halcrow were the consulting engineers. Bristol architect Michael Jenner was engaged to refine the details of the scheme to improve its appearance. He was able to put in some finishing architectural touches to pathways, subways and handrails.

The purpose of the Spine Road was to improve access to businesses and allow the creation of a retail park for *"fun and shopping"* (now Avon Meads and Castle Court), to remove traffic from residential areas and to minimise traffic noise and pollution. As it was going to cross two waterways, power lines, two major roads and five railway lines, the best solution was for much of it to be elevated.

The elevated roadway sits on concrete columns which themselves sit on top of concrete pile foundations extending many metres into the ground. These piles were not, as is usually the case, precast and then driven into the ground, but were formed in–situ from liquid concrete by a method called "vibro–displacement" piling. The ground in St Philips Marsh is soft, and conventional preformed piles are less secure in these conditions. In vibro–displacement piling, a large hollow nozzle around 10m long, and up to 1m wide is "vibrated" into the ground to the required depth. The vibration helps to consolidate the ground. Liquid concrete is then pumped through the nozzle into the surrounding soil, displacing it and allowing a large concrete "bulb" to be formed. The nozzle is slowly raised as more concrete is pumped in. This then

42 | ST PHILIPS CAUSEWAY BRIDGES

forms a concrete column above the bulb which then both solidify, and upon which the above-ground structure can be placed. If needed, a concrete "bulb" can also be formed at the top of the pile to create a wider foundation area. Once the piles at St Philip's Marsh were solid, the precast bridge support columns were placed on them. The prefabricated sections of the viaduct were hoisted into place using a huge 800 tonne "supercrane". Soon after construction, the Cribbs Causeway road and bridges were plagued by defects — the list of problems was said to be 30 pages long, and it wasn't until four years later, after central government agreed to spend £100,000 on remedial work, that the city council agreed to "adopt" the road.

The other major part of the BDC regeneration scheme was a bold project to create a weir in the River Avon which would isolate the river from the tides. It would have allowed the creation of attractive riverside locations and leisure facilities between Bathurst Basin and the tidal limit at Netham. But this depended on funding from the creation of a retail complex near Temple Meads which was never built due to depressed market conditions.

Bristol Development Corporation operated from 1989 to 1994, and was one of 11 Urban Development Corporations (UDC's) set up in major cities by Margaret Thatcher's Conservative Government to regenerate inner city areas using a highly "market-driven" approach. It had a board of directors appointed by the Secretary of State for the Environment and answerable only to him. It was given money and powers to acquire and develop land and was exempted from many local authority constraints. Some saw them as politically motivated undemocratic interventions with no local accountability, imposed on mostly Labour Councils. In Bristol, the Development Corporation was greeted by the then Labour Council with bitter hostility. The results obtained by the UDCs often fell short of the initial promises (surprise!). But the BDC did achieve some of its objectives. It is only now that we are finally seeing some of the things that the BDC wanted to do being brought about by public–private partnerships such as the Local Enterprise Partnership (LEP) that is developing the Temple area. It will still be a few more years before the full vision for east Bristol is realised. As for the bridges, there is little to be said for them aesthetically, and we are still waiting for the weir and its attractive riverbanks.

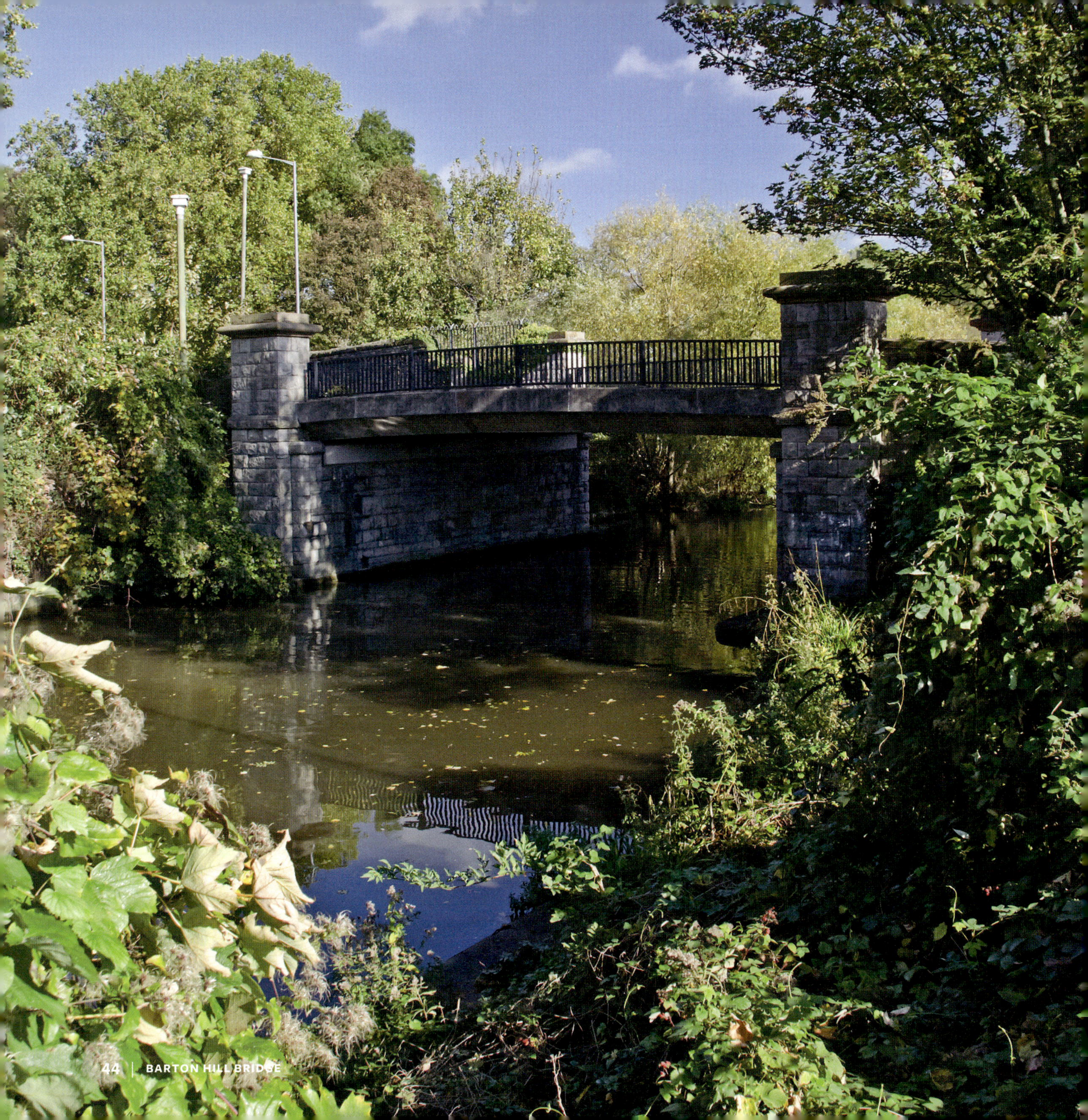

BARTON HILL BRIDGE

Barton Hill Bridge crosses the Feeder Canal, which was an integral part of Willliam Jessop's dock improvement scheme of 1804-9, which created the Floating Harbour. Feeder Canal stretches for 1.6km straight as a die from Marsh Bridge to Netham Lock where it joins the River Avon. When the lock gates are open, fresh riverwater flows into the Feeder and then through the Floating Harbour. Jessop's plan shows a bridge about 200m west of here, so it is likely that this first bridge, undoubtedly wooden, was newly-built with the Feeder. At this time, the land here was fields, farms and open country, so it was probably built for farmers to move cattle and crops over the canal.

By 1840, the first bridge had been replaced with one at the present location and was called Pinney Terrace Bridge, after a row of six terraced houses which been built immediately west of the bridge on the north bank (they no longer exist). They were built by the owners of the nearby Great Western Cotton factory to house some key workers prior to the factory opening in 1838. Charles Pinney was one of the cotton company's directors and lived at the grand Camp House (still there) on Clifton Down Road. He was a West India merchant and slave owner, but just like Colston, at the same time he was a city benefactor and zealous churchman. He became Mayor of Bristol in 1831, just six weeks before the traumatic and destructive weekend of the Bristol Reform Law Riots of that year — some of the worst rioting in the country in the whole of the 19th century. Pinney was put on trial for failing to put down the riots forcefully enough, but was found to have acted with zeal and courage and was aquitted.

By 1899, Pinney Terrace Bridge had become unsafe and had to be closed to vehicles. It was also very inadequate for the demands of the 20th century — it was only 3.7m wide, without a footway and only one vehicle could cross at one time. Around 1900, it was replaced with a fixed bridge having solid sides of flanged steel sheets rivetted together and two roadways separated by a central steel divider. The stone abutments we see today were built at this time. The dark red sandstone cappings, which contrast nicely with the pale limestone walls, are "Wilderness" stone from the Wilderness Quarry at Micheldean in Gloucestershire.

In its turn the the central span was replaced in the late 1960s/early '70s with what we see now — a bridge with open balustrades — which has transformed its appearance from a heavy industrial object to something much lighter in appearance and almost rural were it not for the adjacent busy Feeder Road. In the 20th century, the name Pinney fell out of use and it became known as both Barton Hill Bridge and Marsh Lane Bridge.

When Feeder Canal was completed in 1809, Barton Hill and St Philip's Marsh were still farmland. Barton was a manor just outside Bristol, mentioned in the Domesday Book as Bertune apud Bristov, and later in 1220 as Berton Bristoll. In Saxon and early Norman times the manor was held by the king, and was known as Barton Regis. The manor gave its name to Barton Regis Hundred, and the sloping ground at the southern end of the hundred, leading down to St Philips Marsh, became known as Barton Hill. In the middle ages, several large houses were built here for wealthy Bristol merchants. Barton Hill and St Philip's Marsh remained sleepy rural retreats until the industrial "big bang" of the Victorian Era.

Feeder in Barton Hill.

A Bristol Guide Book of 1874 warns the visitor that in this area lies "*...a gloomy vale enshrouded in almost perpetual smoke... [with] ...works which throw off nauseous gases causing stench laden folds of air to envelop the visitor and make him involuntarily turn to the waterside to try if he can breathe more freely. Innumerable smoke stacks jerk out their filthy fumes which sweep in thick clouds through the streets... enveloping the whole place in an impenetrable stench cloud*". Not that the "waterside" to which the visitor might turn was the slightest bit better. A sample of water taken from near Lysaghts works in 1875 was found to be "*very acid*" and to contain toxic metals. The City Analyst reported that "*this fluid would cause the effervescence of the mud and the evolution of sulphuretted hydrogen and produce the inky appearance observed and the offensive smells so much complained of*" but concluded reassuringly that it was "*not injurious to health per se unless swallowed*".

For nearly two centuries, the Feeder Canal was an essential part of the industrial city. In the 1950s began the de-industrialisation of the whole country. Road and rail transport began to supercede barges and traditional heavy industries went into a long decline. This period also saw the city council taking active steps to move residents out of St Philips Marsh to healthier parts of the city and to demolish the poor quality housing. By the early 1980s, most of the heavy industry around the Feeder and the residential population of St Philip's Marsh had gone.

The decline of heavy industry, combined with increasingly strict environmental laws, has happily seen a reverse in the condition of the Feeder. In the last 50 years, a great deal has been done to rehabilitate it, much of it by voluntary organisations. In 1974, for instance, 120 trees were planted along its length. In the 1970s no living thing could survive in the water, but nowadays it is a popular spot for anglers where you can catch decent sized roach, dace, perch and bream.

Between 1840 and 1880, scores of factories and heavy primary industries sprang up along the whole length of the Feeder on both sides, due to the ease of transporting goods along the canal by barge and its connection to the Port of Bristol. These included iron works, asphalt works, glue works, tanneries and chemical works, ie mostly those industries that were too smelly, noisy, noxious and unpleasant for them to be sited in the centre of the city. Thousands of houses then followed for the workforces. In St Philips the housing was centred south of the Feeder along the western half, around Grafton Street and York Street, and on the north side of the

NETHAM LOCK BRIDGES (East and West)

16 — 19

The Feeder Canal joins the River Avon at Netham Lock and brings fresh water into the Floating Harbour. Here, the level of water in the river is the same as in the Floating Harbour (9.6m above the outer sill of the Entrance Lock at Cumberland Basin) and it is above the reach of most of the tides in the Avon. Tidal water is heavily laden with silt and must be kept out of the Floating Harbour. A build up of silt would reduce the depth of water and cause problems for larger craft (river water does contain silt, but much less than tidal water.) The lock is normally open during the day to allow easy boat access and unrestricted river water flow into the harbour, but it is closed whenever the tide runs

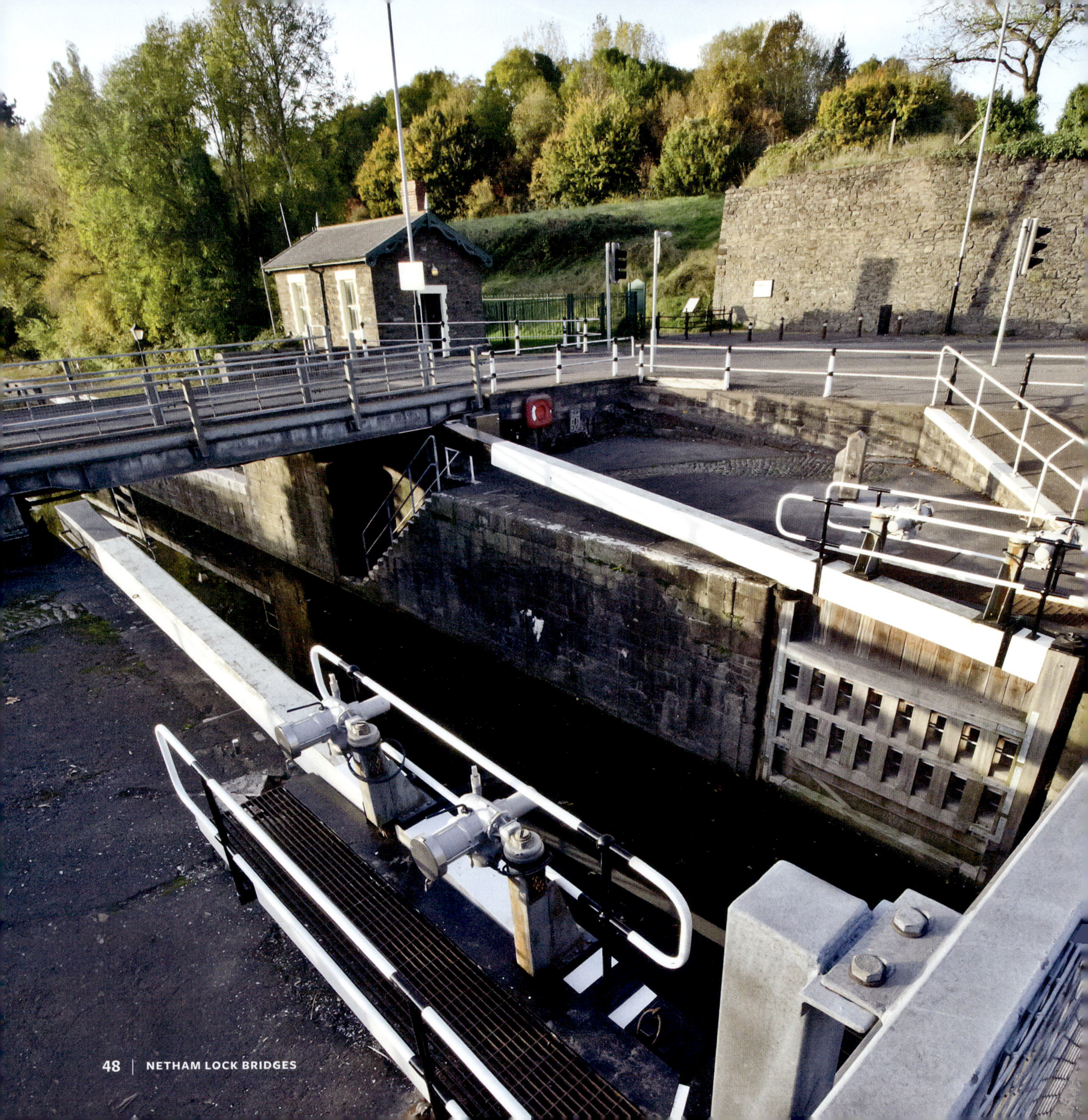

above Netham. A hundred years ago, an almost continuous stream of barges through Netham Lock would have carried raw materials and finished goods to and from the towns and cities linked to Bristol and its port by the country's waterways.

The stone abutments of the west bridge, and the attractive lock keeper's cottage, are part of Jessop's work of 1804-9, so there would have been a low wooden fixed bridge here when the canal was opened. It has been replaced at least twice over the years. A second bridge was added sometime after the 1960s as the volume of tarffic on Netham Road increased with the expansion of Bristol's suburbs around Netham Park. Neither bridge has any noteworthy features.

Up to the middle of the last century, Netham Lock was surrounded by three of Bristol's biggest manufactories. Just to the north, stretching up the hill now occupied by Netham Park, Netham Chemical Works was established in 1859 on 40 acres of land. Five hundred employees manufactured sulphuric acid, caustic soda and washing soda in a sprawling complex of grim industrial structures with a tramway network and a huge waste tip. Crowning it all (until demolished in 1950) was the 'Netham Monster' — a 91m high chimney stack, which stood out as a prominent landmark among a number of other tall chimneys. The factory produced huge amounts of chemical waste, creating a strange landscape of mounds and valleys looking like the surface of the moon. It became a strange unofficial playground for the children of Barton Hill, and it was given the strange name "The Brillos". To the west (downstream) of the chemical works stood the Great Western Cotton Factory established in 1838 — the biggest cotton factory outside the north-west, employing nearly 1,000 people. To the south side of the lock, on 13 acres of land once known as Feeder Farm, came Lysaght's Engineering Works in 1876, eventually stretching over 400m from here to Barton Hill Bridge. Here were manufactured many of the bridges which span the city's waterways as well as constructional ironwork for churches, railway stations and warehouses.

The Chemical Works closed in 1949, the Cotton Factory was demolished in the 1960s and Lysaght's Netham Works closed in 1970. The whole area of the chemical works, including the spoil heaps, have been reclaimed and utterly transformed to produce the lovely Netham Park and a pleasant tree lined canal-side walk. St Vincent's Trading Estate is now on the site of John Lysaght's Steel Works.

NEW BRISLINGTON BRIDGE

A bridge was first erected here in 1890 *"to open up property about to be developed on the Somerset side near to the village of Brislington"*. It was a bowstring lattice steel girder type and was paid for by the firm who designed and built it, John Lysaght Ltd, who had a major engineering works close by on the banks of the Feeder Canal. There was probably a high degree of self-interest at work, as the company would now find it easier to recruit workers from Brislington (most of whom, in those days, would be walking or cycling to work) and whose "commute" would now be considerably shortened. The bridge was known as Lysaghts Bridge until it was replaced by the current concrete bowstring bridge around 1936–38, which was then known as New Brislington Bridge. It is austere but certainly imposing.

"New Brislington" was the name originally given to this area as the village of Brislington expanded northwards at the beginning of the 20th century. Apart from this bridge, the name has now disappeared from the map and the area is now regarded as on the edge of St Annes.

The 1930s bridge was part of Neville Chamberlain's "five-year plan" for the improvement of roads and bridges throughout the country. It was also one of the unemployment relief schemes that the city council implemented to alleviate the severe economic depression of the interwar years, when the unemployment rate never dropped below 10 percent and peaked at over 20 percent. The welfare system was then in its infancy, and although most workers were covered by a national insurance scheme, unemployment benefit was limited to four months per year and six weeks' contributions were required to get one week's benefit. When jobs were so scarce for such a long period, there were many people who were never able to make contributions and were unable to get benefit. Millions were in poverty. Local councils implemented job creation projects for which government grants were usually available. Bristol City Council proudly proclaimed that it ran 119 such schemes between 1920 and 1932.

Although this was Bristol's first concrete bridge, such bridges were first used in the late 19th century. In the early 20th century, reinforced concrete bridges came on the scene and by the time of this bridge they were pretty commonplace. The city councillors had a choice between this and a steel bridge, and chose concrete because it was cheaper.

As you cross the bridge you have a good view of Netham Wier, a few hundred metres downstream. This is an important part of the system that controls the level and flow of water into the Floating Harbour.

The Romans invented concrete. Look up as you pass the middle of the bridge — is it too far fetched for the rough uprights of this economical offering to put one in mind of classical columns and ruined Roman temples?

NEW BRISLINGTON BRIDGE | 51

ST ANNE'S FOOTBRIDGE

As you stand at this now unremarkable spot, it is hard to believe that for centuries this location was once of national importance. About 200m south of this bridge used to stand the small shrine of St Anne's Chapel, built possibly in the 12th century (long since vanished without trace), which was a site of religious pilgrimage in the mediaeval period, perhaps of equal significance to Canterbury and Walsingham. St Anne is the patron saint of sailors, ports and harbours. Crusaders returning from the Holy Land gave holy relics to the chapel and the secular wealthy donated art and antiquities. It is recorded that 32 model ships hung from the rafters. The Chapel was visited by Henry VII in 1498 and then by his queen a few years later, in 1502. An annual commemorative walk to the ancient and extant St Anne's Well in nearby St Anne's Woods, long associated with the pilgrimage, has been revived by local residents.

It was only in 1950s that the footbridge you now walk over replaced a wooden ferry boat which had been operating perhaps for 850 years — originally ferrying pilgims arriving on the route from the north to the shrine close by the south bank. St. Anne's ferry formed part of the manor of Blackswarth and was owned by the monastery of St Augustine, Bristol. After the dissolution of the monasteries the ferry was taken over by the the Crown and was let to a private operator at a rent of one shilling (five pence) per annum.

The south bank at St Anne's had a second dose of fame in the 20th century when the St Annes Board Mill Company built the giant St Anne's Board Mills there in 1912, with a 30m high chimney, to make cardboard packaging, mainly for the tobacco industry. The company also bought the operating rights to the ferry and for about 40 years it was worked by three uniformed employees of the mills from 5.30am untill 10.30pm. In 1957, the company built this footbridge and closed down the ferry. In the 1970s, the factory was producing 160,000–170,000 tonnes of cardboard per annum and employing 1,800 people — they had become one of the top three boardmakers in the UK. Economic circumstances forced closure in 1980, and just like St Anne's Chapel, of the factory nothing now remains. The site is now mainly housing.

The footbridge is a simple fixed steel truss type which would be rather ordinary were it not for the contrasting colour of the diagonal cross bracing. Seen a little way away from the side, it looks like a compressed spring ready to jump out. No doubt a happy accident, it gives the bridge a feeling of stored energy waiting for release.

ST ANNE'S FOOTBRIDGE | 53

54 | FEEDER CANAL FOOTBRIDGE

FEEDER CANAL FOOTBRIDGE

The last decades of the 19th century saw the area around the Feeder Canal transformed from open green fields to dense heavy industry with a large resident population. Housing centered on Barton Hill on the north side. South of the Feeder, there were houses on Feeder Road itself (on the south side), next to Marsh Bridge. The majority in St Philips lived in the streets of closely-packed terraced houses between Victoria Road and Atlas Terrace. Most had no bathrooms or indoor toilets. Despite the hard conditions, there was a good community spirit and sense of pride.

People and goods in quantity now needed to constantly criss-cross the Feeder. In the 1890s, the only crossing points were Marsh Bridge, at the west end, and Pinney Terrace Bridge (now Barton Hill Bridge) to the east, which meant at least a 0.75km walk for most of the inhabitants of St Philip's Marsh. Since 1867, the church of St Silas-in-the-Marsh had stood 150m to the west of the present footbridge at the corner of Arthur Street. In January 1896, the Bristol press reported that the vicar, Rev F J Horsefield, was agitating about the fact that he had a parish of 8,000 people that was split in two by the Feeder. Two years earlier, the city council, already aware of the problems, had tried to buy land for the approaches to a new bridge but the landowners, the Great Western Railway (GWR), refused to sell, and there the matter rested. In July 1896, a petition for a bridge (organised, I suspect, by Rev Horsefield) was signed by 700 people including himself, the vicar of St Lukes in Barton Hill and some local prominent provision of a staircase on Feeder Road. At long last, tenders went out in 1900. Messrs Krauss, who were a Bristol Builder and Contractor, got the job. The footbridge was finally opened without ceremony on 24th June 1901. The span is still the original (note the rivets) but the steps are a recent replacement.

The years 1873–1896 saw a worldwide economic recession, the "Long Depression", sparked off by a global financial panic (sound familiar?). It was longest and most severe in Europe and the United States, but the UK is thought to have been the hardest hit, with high unemployment and great social hardship. At that time, these were regarded as problems to be sorted out by charity, not government policy. In 1896, Rev. Horsefield was stirring things up not just about bridges. He invited a journalist from the Bristol Mercury to tour his parish with him. The result was an article in the Mercury in April that year headed *"Suffering in St Silas"*. The writing from this anonymous journalist is worthy of Dickens, but this was not fiction and is still heartrending to read, more than 100 years later:

"People have put up houses in all sorts of awkward positions in narrow roads leading nowhere devoid of footways. The Sanitary Authority has set its mark in two ways on the parish… at its eastern extremity it has built the destructor for the refuse and on the other extremity is the unwelcome Fever Hospital…. In between, what was once a rural district has been cut up by railway embankments, manufactories with tall chimneys and spoil heaps. Odours from the… chimneys were most baleful. Large families… live in 2 roomed houses…packed back to back (where) young lives are ushered into sorrow. On a dull damp day, a thick black cloud settles over the place and the atmosphere is well-nigh suffocating. The finest buildings are the public houses of which there are 26. In one street, 335 persons were crowded into 62 houses. I was shown a miserable little cottage where a woman fish hawker had brought up a family of 6. She is now aged and dependent on her son…who for a whole week had nothing but a half slice of bread a day. What

business people. This seems to have nudged things on, because by the following autumn the GWR had agreed to sell the land required to connect Silverthorne Lane with Feeder Road by a bridge. Another problem then arose — the levels on the two sides of the Feeder at this point are very different, and a roadbridge would need considerably more land and earthworks. After further delay it was decided to build a footbridge only, as this would only require the

sort of appetite must it give [...to the vicar..] to have a message that a parishioner is dying, and to be told by the doctor that it is more starvation than anything else."

The *"Condition of the Working Class in England"*, specifically parts of Bristol in 1896, was evidently no better than when Frederick Engels, patron of Karl Marx, was recording his own observations in Manchester 50 years earlier in his book of that name.

Five years after the church of St Silas was consecrated, it began to show signs of subsidence due to the spongy nature of the subsoil (the area wasn't called St Philip's *Marsh* for nothing). It got so bad that, in the end, the church had to be closed and demolished in March 1872. The foundation stone of a new church was laid later that year. The new church opened in August, 1878. It was destroyed by a German incendiary bomb in 1941 and not rebuilt.

MARSH BRIDGE

MARSH BRIDGE

Marsh Bridge was one of the original bridges built by Jessop for his Floating Harbour scheme, completed in 1809. As the Feeder Canal was only used by small craft and barges it was probably a low, fixed timber bridge. By 1861, it was in poor condition and was replaced by something similar. Some 40 years later, at the turn of the century, it was again in poor condition and had become too narrow for modern needs. Another replacement was therefore carried out in 1910, this time using steel. The bridge was widened and an adjoining footbridge was added on the east side. At that time there was a considerable amount of foot traffic across the bridge arising from dense housing in the vicinity on the south side of Feeder Road, and the proximity of the Rising Sun pub a few metres to the north. The bridge we see now, little more than a flat concrete slab of road with railings, is a further replacement carried out in the 1960s.

Fifteen minutes of fame for Marsh Bridge arrived on Wednesday, 9th October 1889, at around 6pm when, by happenstance, it was at the epicentre of one of Bristol's first mass trade union disputes.

In 1872 it ceased to be a crime to be a member of a Trade Union. Working conditions in late Victorian times were grim, work was hard and the hours long. Most people worked 52 weeks a year. At first it was mainly skilled craftsmen who formed unions. They were quite small organisations and were not inclined to be very militant. However, in the late 1880's membership spread amongst unskilled and semi-skilled workers such as dockers, miners and cotton workers. Women also were joining in significant numbers. Out of the blue came the Great Strike Wave of 1889–1890, when the whole of the UK was hit by an unprecedented number of strikes chiefly organised by the Unions of the semi-skilled and unskilled, rather than the older craft unions. Bristol was no exception. Striking groups included gas workers, dockers, stay makers, cotton workers, brush makers, hatters, pipe makers, coal carriers, street cleaners, box makers, cigar makers, tramway men, hauliers, bargemen, and charcoal workers. The city's labour historian Samuel Bryher depicted Bristol at this time as *"a seething centre of revolt"*.

The gasworkers' strike was one of Bristol's first big strikes. At that time, gas was produced by burning coal, and as electricity was in its infancy, gas was the chief source of power and light for the city — a key industry. Most of the work done by Bristol's 600 gasworkers was heavy manual labour, such as shovelling coal by hand into the kilns. They were employed by the Bristol United Gas and Light Company in three gasworks in the city, the main one being on Avon Street, near Marsh Bridge. During the summer of 1889, the Gasworkers Union had submitted a wage claim and other demands to the management which had been rebuffed. A strike was called for 9th October and the company was given a week's notice. This allowed the company management time to arrange for around 300 substitute workers ("blacklegs" in Trade Union terms) from various cities as far away as Liverpool to be brought to Bristol by train on the first day of the strike. From Temple Meads station they were to be taken in horse drawn open wagons to the three gasworks where accommodation and food had been organised. The management omitted, however, to inform these unfortunates that they would be strikebreakers and that they would be likely to receive a somewhat cool reception from the workers they would be replacing. Some, having been told they would be working in new factories, and expecting to stay for some time, brought their wives and children. The Bristol Mercury was sympathetic to the workers' cause and remarkably scathing about the company: *"the directors... have maintained an attitude of mystery and secrecy better suited to comic opera conspirators... They have not offered an explanation of the men's complaint.... The [company] manager... seems to have imagined... [the strikebreakers]... would be conveyed to the works... as readily as a gentleman driving in his hansom [carriage] to his hotel. Such childlike confidence nearly led to a catastrophe for which the wilful ignorance of the company would have made them culpably responsible... we trust they will stop short of a crowning blunder"*.

On the day of the strike, virtually the whole 600-strong workforce took to the streets outside the company's three works, some singing "Britons never will be slaves" with bystanders joining in. Avon Street was crowded by 1pm as men coming out of the Gasworks were cheered by workers from nearby factories. This scene was repeated at the other works in Canons Marsh and Stapleton. The strikers were aware of the imminent arrival by train of strikebreakers. Marsh bridge, at the bottom of Avon Street, and which the strikebreakers would have to cross to get to the gasworks there, was packed with people. Sympathetic boatmen had barricaded it with carts and wagons to form an impenetrable barrier. Meanwhile, a crowd of strikers and supporters numbering "thousands" assembled inside Temple Meads station waiting for the trains bringing in the strikebreakers.

At about 5.30pm, the first train arrived with around 120 men from Exeter. A contingent of 50 policemen managed to get them through the seething hostile crowd inside the station into eight or nine horse-drawn vehicles and they set off along Cattlemarket Road towards Marsh Bridge and the Avon Street works. The road was lined with people hooting and using language of *"no very choice kind"*. When the first vehicle was close to the bridge *"excited women"* began to throw stones. More joined in. The strike leaders did what they could to prevent violence — thankfully largely effective — and spoke to the strikebreakers about the folly of trying to get across Marsh Bridge. Scuffles broke out, resulting in a few black eyes, but eventually all the incomers returned to the station in the wagons protesting ignorance of the strike. Had the police not been very restrained the results could have been a lot worse.

Similar scenes occurred near St Philip's Bridge on the north side of the station: this time the strikebreakers disappeared into the crowds. Soon all the new arrivals had returned to Temple Meads station where they were guarded by a large body of police. until they could get on trains to take them home.

In a small but potentially serious incident in Avon Street, a horse-drawn cab drew up around 5pm. Three men got out and there was a scuffle involving a policeman. A revolver was drawn, and a shot was fired that made a hole in the brim of a hat worn by a young man in the vicinity. The cab was overturned, arrests were made.

In the early evening, it was estimated by the Bristol Mercury that there were some 15,000 people — men, women, youths and children, congregating in St Philips. Several thousand of these were inside the station waiting for trains bringing more strikebreakers from Hereford, Newport and Liverpool. Each time a train arrived, a compact mass of bodies — workers, supporters, bystanders, policemen and terrified ordinary passengers caught up in the melee — surged towards it and a huge angry roar went up with cries of *"don't get out"*, *"there's a strike"* *"you'll be killed"*, which must have struck terror in those inside the trains. Once again, when the situation was explained to the incomers, they all agreed to return home, some wishing the strikers good luck. By around 10pm, the station crowd had dwindled to a few hundred and the day's excitement was over. Within the next 24 hours, the management conceded most of the strikers demands and the strike was settled.

The gasworkers' strike ended relatively free of violence. In the even bigger strikes and demonstrations which were to follow in Bristol over the next few months, the police and the military would respond with much more force. A new kind of history had begun.

MARSH BRIDGE | 61

TOTTERDOWN BRIDGE

On Ashmead's Map of Bristol, published in 1874, Pylle Hill is already densely built over with housing but there is still completely open land south and east of St Lukes Road and what would become St Johns Lane. From that date on, up to the turn of the century, Totterdown grew rapidly eastwards, more than doubling in size to that which we know today. Most of the inhabitants worked north of the river, increasingly in the industries that were being established in St Philip's Marsh. But it was a 2.5km walk there from Totterdown via Bath Bridge.

A petition for a footbridge linking St Philip's Marsh

to Totterdown gathered 400–500 signatures and had been handed to the city council in February 1880. It seemed that the council had agreed to put the matter in hand. But a year later, with no apparant progress being made, a meeting was held at St Silas School in St Philip's Marsh in order to put pressure on the council to get on with it. It was attended by interested councillors and local worthies. William Brock (he of Brock's Bridge, see chapter 9), who was the owner of a large joinery and building business on St Philip's Marsh next to the river, proposed the motion, which was carried, that a bridge be provided between Totterdown and the Marsh. Someone made reference to a previous attempt at getting a bridge built here 35 years earlier, and another cautioned that they... *"must not expect this bridge to be put up in a month or two months"*. Wise words, for the construction of this particular Bristol bridge was attended with more fraught debate, complications and delays than any other bridge in the city to date, with the exception of the Clifton Suspension Bridge. Paradoxically, Mr Brock eventually ended up himself delaying the opening of the bridge to vehicles by 12 months or more.

Just two weeks before the St Silas meeting, a fatal acccident had occurred involving an unlicenced ferry operating at the point where Totterdown Bridge now stands, which perhaps helped to concentrate the minds of the city fathers on the fact that rowing boat ferries were by no means a benign, risk–free mode of transport. Three men were being carried over the river by the ferryman when the chain used to pull the boat across the water snapped against a very strong tide. The boat was swamped, and the ferryman and a passenger were immediately thrown out. Though they struggled hard to get to the shore, they both drowned. The other two passengers clung to the semi–submerged boat as it rapidly drifted downriver. One swam ashore near Bath Bridge, and the third was rescued by another boat near Vauxhall Bridge.

A considerable period of debate then ensued within

the council about the proposed bridge. Where to place the bridge precisely? Two locations were mooted. Should it be a footbridge or a vehicle carriageway costing double that amount? Should it be a high level bridge at the level of Bath Road, or a low level bridge with an incline to Bath Road? It took five years, after engineers' reports and costings, before a decision was made: the bridge was to be a high level vehicular bridge sited where the ferry had operated. Noteworthy contributions from local councillors to the debate were:

"Totterdown, like the Marsh, had not had a shilling of the city's money spent on it in improvements — and in this bridge they intend to have the first instalment."

"....[the bridge] would permit the people of St Philips to take a walk in the country."

"...the people were not aesthetic, and did not mind the bridge being ugly, so long as they would have it useful".

Further delays ensued. Unsuccessful attempts were made by the council to obtain contributions to the cost from property owners whose land value would increase as a result of the new bridge. An Act of Parliament had to be passed, due to the complication that St Philip's Marsh was in Bristol and Totterdown was in Somerset — two different authorities. Then another problem arose. The aforementioned Mr Brock operated a single business from two separate but proximate yards on the north bank. The landowner had allowed him to put down a short stretch of rail track to move goods by tram between the two yards. The council had purchased the land between the two yards for the new approach road to the bridge but the required road gradient rendered Mr Brock's tramway impossible. There was the matter of compensation for Mr Brock to be addressed.

Tenders for the bridge went out in early 1888. Bristol builder Mr Solomon Turner, of Stapleton Road, won the contract for the masonry and Messrs. John Lysaght Ltd that for the steelwork. By June of that year, construction was underway. The bridge was completed and opened in early 1889, but at first only to pedestrians. This was because Mr Brock was now in legal dispute with the council over the issue of compensation for infringing his right of way between his yards. This prevented the use of the Albert Road approach by vehicular traffic until the following year. Total time from intial successful petition to opening of bridge: 10 years. Did the inhabitants of Totterdown get an "ugly" bridge? Not quite — the stonework is attractive — but the huge collection of pipework under the steelwork is not. Let's call it "utilitarian".

As the new bridge was nearing completion, the Great Western Railway announced their intention to build the Temple Meads Relief Line Bridge (see chapter 11), 400m downstream. The city council decided to take advantage of getting a bridge on the cheap by paying the company for the extra cost of adding a footbridge to it. For the citizens of Totterdown, it was a case of waiting 10 years for a bridge and then two come along all at once!

LANGTON ST BRIDGE (Banana Bridge)

Langton Street footbridge was put in place (I choose those words carefully) **in 1882.** It was designed by the Borough Engineer, Mr. Ashmead, and made by Edward Finch and Co, of Chepstow, for £1,800.

Edward Finch and Co were initially based in Liverpool, but set up a works in Chepstow to construct the Chepstow Railway Bridge for Brunel in 1852 using innovative tubular girders, later copied by him at Saltash Bridge. After this work was completed, Finch remained in Chepstow, and developed a major engineering and shipbuilding business on the site.

The bridge's initial fabrication and location, however, was not Langton Street. It was constructed two years earlier at the site of Bedminster Bridge as a temporary replacement for the old Bedminster Bridge whilst a new one was being built. When that bridge was finished, this one was moved to the Langton Street site. The ingenious way it was moved was by floating it upstream on four 80 tonne barges. The barges were fixed together as two pairs, each of which had one half of a timber superstructure constructed on top of it around 7m high. This preliminary work was carried out in the floating harbour and took three weeks. When the day came to move the footbridge, a crowd of several thousand gathered at 6am to watch. The two pairs of barges were positioned under the bridge at low tide and bolted together to make a single

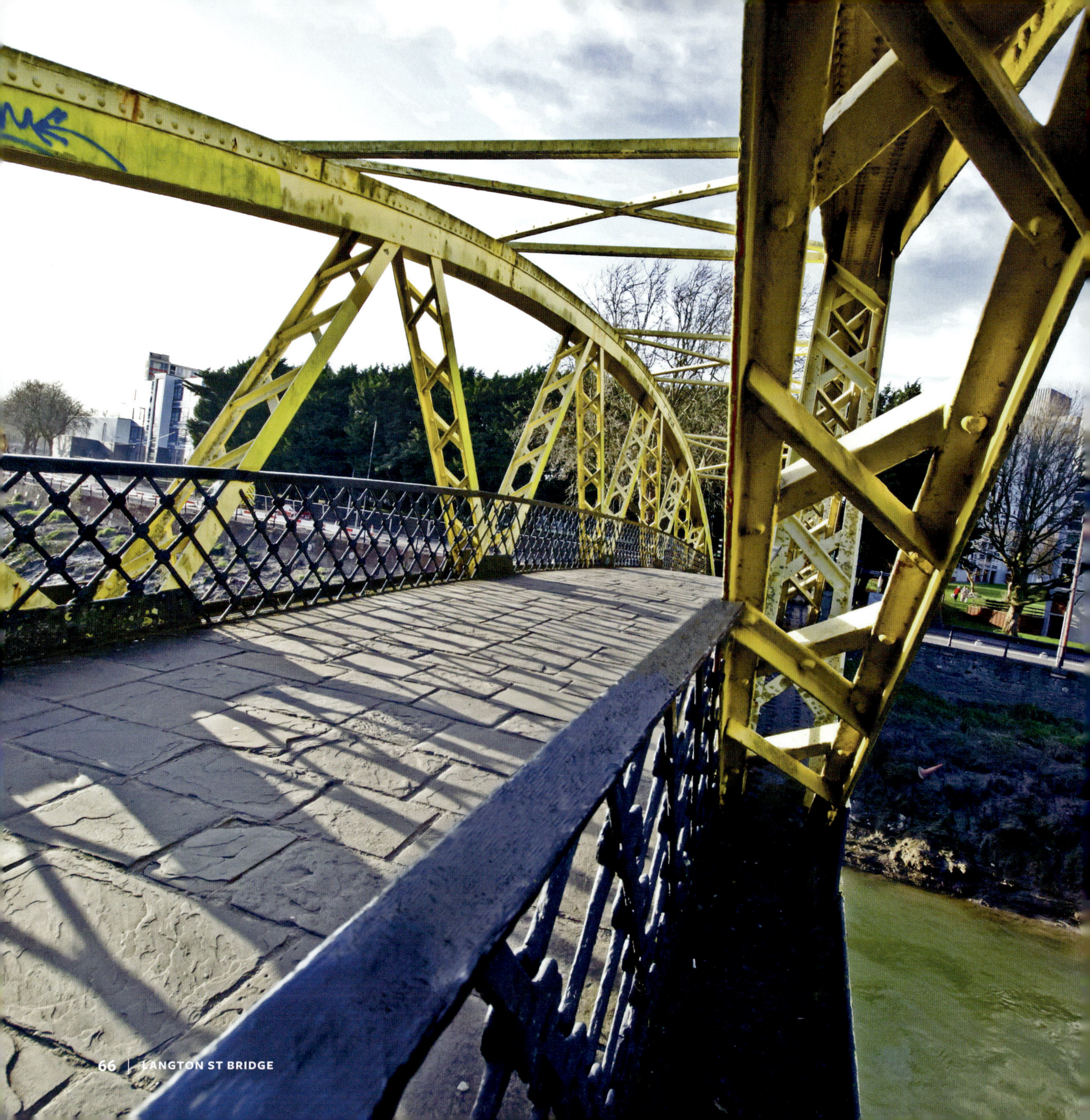

supporting structure. As the tide rose, the rising structure lifted it off the abutments, and the barges plus bridge were turned through 90 degrees to be towed upstream for 30 mins to Langton Street, forming *"a graceful and majestic sight towering above the banks of the river"*. As the tide fell the bridge was guided into position — to within 1.6mm — on the new abutments. A *"long desired and much needed"* new crossing point.

It is a basic steel "bowstring" truss bridge with diagonal braces and crossed railings. That which lifts its appearance a little above the ordinary is the repetition of the curve of the bow in the upward curve of the deck, turning what would otherwise be a pretty mundane design into something much lighter and elegant in appearance. In recent years, the shape has earned it the "banana" nickname. The steelwork rests on substantial "battered" (angled back) abutments of Pennant sandstone built by W. Galbraith, of Nova Scotia Yard, Bristol. The decking comprises stone flags of the same material — an unusual choice, given the added weight of stone compared to timber. Pennant stone is a tough medium-to-coarse grained local sandstone from the Carboniferous Coal Measures, and widely used in Bristol for buildings, paving, and stone abutments in the 19th and 20th centuries. It can have a range of colours, mostly greyish with a blue or green cast, but sometimes it can be a strong plum-red or yellow ochre. When the colours are randomly combined, it can look very attractive. It is often, as here, used with the exposed surface roughly finished, called "rustication", in order to give a feeling of strength and stability to the construction as a whole.

Around 20 years ago, the city council gave Langton Street Bridge a paint job to match its fruity nickname. I am grateful to the lady in the matching yellow mac who happened to walk into the frame of the main photo just as I was about to press the shutter. A complementary print of this photo awaits her if she would care to get in touch.

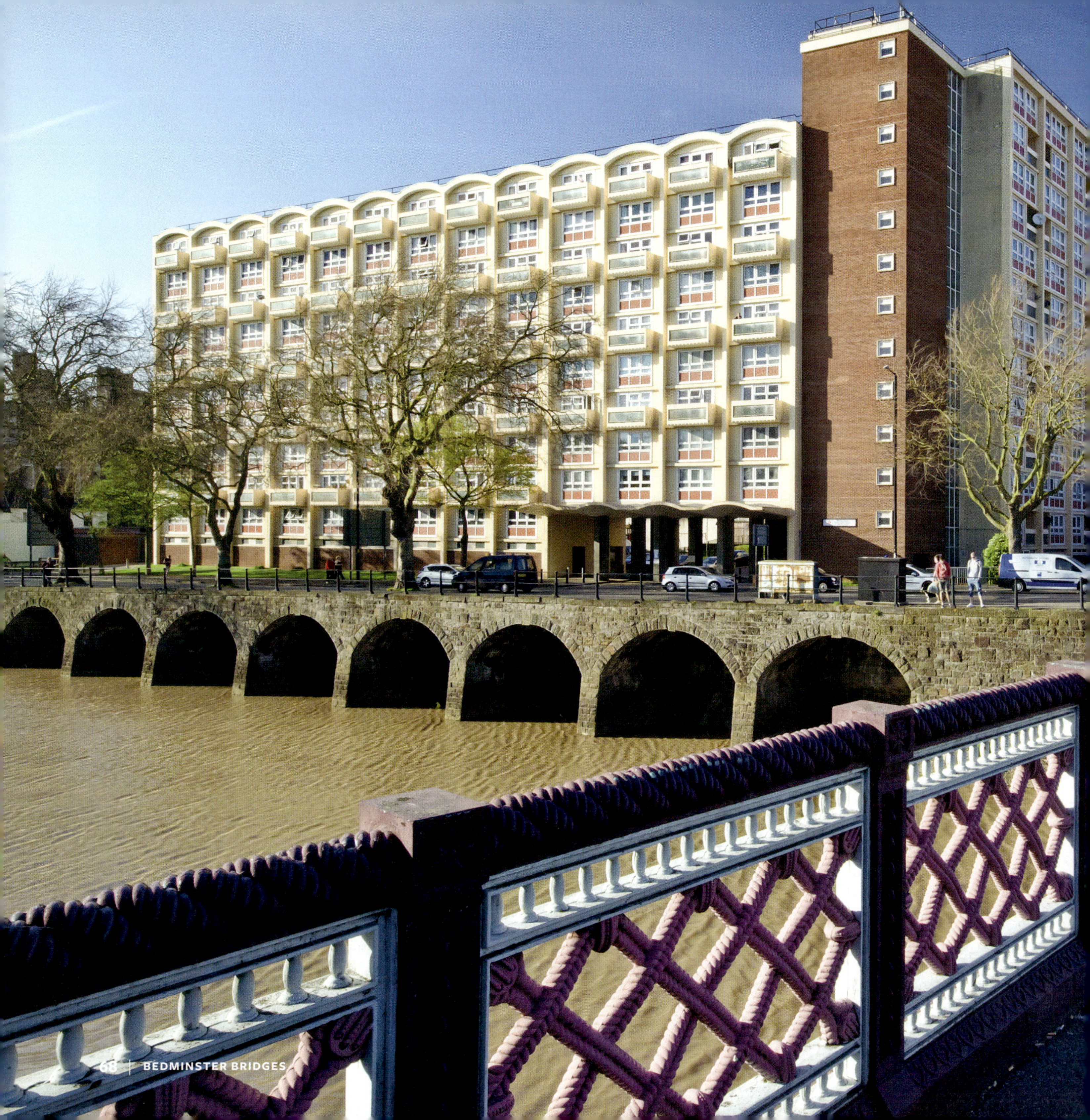

BEDMINSTER BRIDGES

(East and West)

The current bridge is a listed grade II structure, dates from 1883, and cost £16,000. In the 1960s, it was doubled with an uninteresting concrete bridge 50m to the east, creating a roundabout.

The first bridge, built where the western bridge now stands, was the cast–iron Harford's Bridge of 1809, named after John Scandrett Harford, banker and owner/financier of the Blaise Castle Estate. This bridge was identical and contemporaneous with Hill's Bridge (where Bath Bridge now stands). They were both designed by William Jessop and made by the Coalbrokedale Company of Ironbridge. Each comprised a series of six slender arched ribs of cast iron, parallel with each other 2m apart, resting on stone abutments. The arched ribs supported vertical cast iron pillars that supported the road deck. The use of iron for bridge construction was still a rarity at this time.

Its sister bridge did not survive a collision with a barge in 1855 which caused its complete collapse. Harford's Bridge was luckier — in October 1860, an African trader ship, the "*Fanny Chapman*"*, went out of control on a high tide. The bowsprit struck the pavement and balustrade of the crowded bridge and the bridge shook as the ship bounced off but it stayed standing. No one was injured.

Harford's Bridge was demolished in 1882 — by then it was too narrow for the traffic and was regarded as a relic from Bristol's agricultural past, although the then city

---

*Fanny Chapman was a member of the local gentry – her diaries can be found online.

dock engineer Thomas Howard praised its bold, skilful and handsome design. It was temporarily replaced with the bridge that was subsequently moved about two years later, by floating it upstream, to become the Langton Street Bridge.

The abutments here are of the ubiquitous local Pennant sandstone. The single span has a shallow elliptical arch. What really distinguishes Bedminster Bridge is its magnificent ornamental cast-ironwork made by Cochrane and Co of Dudley, which has been highlighted by a superb paint scheme. On the sides of the arch, there is a cross lattice pattern with "bosses" of flowers set between vertical chains. The balustrades consist of interwoven ropes beneath a heavy rope handrail.

If you stand at the south end of the bridge and look northwest, you have an impressive urban landscape in front of you. The backdrop is the Waring House towerblock (1958–60), a fine example of Corbusier-style late English Modernism. The scalloped roofline of this building facing the river echoes the ancient-looking arched stone revetments which support the roadway on the river bank.

BATHURST BASIN FOOTBRIDGE

Bathurst Basin was constructed in 1809 as part of Jessop's Floating Harbour scheme but was not fully developed until the 1860s, when warehouses and transit sheds were built here. The former warehouse and offices of Robinsons Oil Seed Manufactory to the north end of the west quay (look for the oriental–looking pointed windows), dates from 1874 and is a splendid example of the so–called "Bristol Byzantine" style popular in the Victorian period. The imposing mass of the former Bristol General Infirmary (1859), now residential, stands on the opposite side of the basin on the site of the former John Acraman's ironworks, which specialised in anchors and chains, and later shipbuilding.

The current footbridge was preceded by two previous bridges. First was a hand–operated simple two–leaf wooden swing bridge built when the basin was constructed. It was replaced in 1872 by a combined railway and footbridge of the bascule (counterweighted lifting) type, raised by steam power, built for the new Bristol Harbour Railway. This joint venture by the Great Western Railway (GWR) and its sister company, the Bristol and Exeter Railway, brought goods trains into the Floating Harbour for the first time. The railway initially ran from Temple Meads station, through a tunnel underneath Redcliffe Hill, over the bascule bridge and stopped at Bathurst Basin. The route was extended within a few years to Princes Wharf and Wapping Wharf 800m to the west. The railway bridge was removed in 1963 but the railway cutting and tunnel entrance (bricked up) can still be seen from the bridge on the north side of Lower Guinea Street, and there are still some railway tracks set in the cobbles on the east quay a few yards south of here. The steam engine that raised the bridge was also used to manouvre boats by means of ropes running around pulleys that still exist on the quay edge near Lower Guinea Street. The engine house was demolished in 1964 and the engine was placed in Bristol's Industrial Museum, now M Shed.

On 21st November 1888, the Bathurst Basin railway/footbridge was engulfed in one of the most spectacular, though tragic, disasters ever to happen in the centre of a British city. The day before, an unprecedentedly large quantity, some 300 barrels, of naptha had been loaded onto the ketch *"United"*, with a crew of four, in Welsh Back. After loading, it moored overnight on the west quay of Bathurst Basin. Naptha is a colourless, volatile and extremely flammable liquid, obtained from the distillation of crude oil, very similar to petrol. The fire and explosion hazards of naptha were quite well understood at the time — there was some legislation, albeit patchy, controlling its transport and storage. At about 11.20 am on the morning in question, the river policeman who was supervising the transit of the cargo had just finished talking to one of the the crew who mentioned a very strong smell of naptha below deck — though he had not seen any leaks. As the policeman turned and walked away from the boat there was a gigantic explosion which shook the ground like an earthquake. The boat turned into a fireball and burning naptha spread out over the basin causing it to become a *"mass of living fire"*. Smoke, flames and burning timbers shot up more than 50 feet into the air and higher than the imposing corner tower of the infirmary. Three crew members perished instantly. The fourth was blown into the water and later rescued with just a broken leg. Every pane of glass, (around 1,000 in total), in the infirmary facade facing the basin was shattered as were all the windows in Robinsons warehouse on Bathurst quay. Amazingly, no one inside was hurt. A huge pall of black smoke and flames obscured the hospital from view. At one point, flames entered the building, blistered a door and set fire to some curtains but quick action from the staff put them out. The wood frames of some of Robinson's windows caught fire but were similarly exinguished. The patients in their beds on the basin side of the hospital were, of course, terrified, but the infirmary staff did a stirling job of getting them to safety. One patient was observed walking briskly away from the scene with his crutches tucked underneath his arm.

The explosion was heard in many parts of the city. Much of the southwest of it was affected by the smoke cloud. A large crowd of onlookers formed. Those standing in Coronation Road found the heat to be almost unbearable. Fire-fighting teams arrived and began directing water on the surrounding buildings and the railway bridge. Burning barrels of naptha floated up and clustered at the bridge, whose ironwork became almost red hot. Water that was being jetted onto the bridge hissed and spat and turned into steam which added to the murk in the air. The railway track buckled and some of the bridge ironwork curled up into grotesque shapes. Some of the substantial woodwork forming the pedestrian deck caught fire. It looked as if the bridge might be destroyed. One fireman chopped away at the smouldering timbers wielding his "...*ponderous axe [with] vigorous blows [which] made the bridge resound and the splinters fly and gained for him the approving remarks of the onlookers.*" After 30 mins of fire-fighting, the bridge was saved, but about 50m of the wharf stonework was calcined and turned crumbly. The fire burned itself out by mid-afternoon and the danger was over.

At the subsequent inquiry, there was no firm evidence about the cause. It was concluded that it was most likely that enough naptha vapours had seeped from the barrels and accumulated in the unventilated hold to form an explosive concentration. One of the crew members had perhaps struck a match for a smoke which ignited the vapours. The City Docks Authority and the consignor of the goods were criticised for allowing the cargo to be put aboard a vessel totally unsuitable for it, although at the time there were no regulations covering this. The Docks Authority quickly prohibited any further shipments of naptha through the harbour and suppliers changed the containers from wooden barrels to steel tanks.

During the 1970s, the Bathurst Basin area was becoming derelict. A developer proposed replacing the old industrial buildings between the harbour and Bathurst Basin with housing. With a mind to regenerate the area, the city council made the provision, by the developer, of a new footbridge to replace the former railway bridge a condition of planning consent. The developer jibbed at the cost. In an early example of recycling ethos, Bristol Civic Society commissioned Bristol engineer Richard Fenton to design a footbridge using redundant steel tubes used for dredging operations at Avonmouth. Fenton had to accomodate two constraints: only one size of tube was available and the project was intended to be a job creation scheme (thereby attracting a grant) and would be assembled by people with little training. Fenton's design came in at about half the price originally quoted by the developer, and was accepted. But by the time the bridge was eventually built, in 1985, the unwanted steel tubes were long gone. New tubes had to be used — putting the cost back up again! Nevertheless, it was built. As the bridge had already been designed using just one tube size, that is how it was made with new tubes. This new bridge signified an important moment in the history of Floating Harbour — the end of the industrial era and the beginning of the era of leisure and pleasure.

BATHURST BASIN ROADBRIDGES (East and West)

This pair of bridges stand at the south end of Bathust Basin, which began life in the middle ages as a millpond for Trin (or Treen) Mill. Pond and mill were constructed by the nearby St. Augustine's Abbey (now Bristol Cathedral) in the late-12th century. The north end of Bathurst Basin is roughly at the spot where the River Malago, which fed the mill pond after flowing north through Bedminster, used to enter the River Avon before the latter was diverted into the New Cut in 1809. The New Cut radically changed the appearance of this area, truncating the Malago, which now flows into the "new" course of the river some distance south of here. The pond lay to the south of the mill and was irregular in shape, with a large central island. With the construction of the New Cut, the

Malago disappeared at this point and the mill pond became a connecting basin, through two sets of locks, between the Floating Harbour to the north and the River Avon in the New Cut to the south. The connection enabled smaller vessels to bypass the main entrance locks in Cumberland Basin. Eventually, the basin was surrounded by a mixture of warehouses and residences.

The first bridge here was a double-leaf timber swing bridge with lattice-work railings, and was part of the construction of the basin in 1804–9. It was replaced around 1877 with a hand-operated wrought iron swing bridge built by Hennet, Spink and Else, of Bridgwater, which had previously been installed in 1863 over William Jessop's North Entrance Lock in Cumberland Basin. It was removed from there after only a few years' service, when that lock was enlarged in the 1860s.

This bridge was, in turn, replaced by the existing workaday steel swing bridge (it no longer swings) made by Findlay and Co in 1905–6. The ability to swing was controversial. It was a moot point whether the extra expense was justified for the relatively little traffic that used the basin at that time.

The south lock of the basin was blocked at the beginning of World War Two to ensure that, in case of damage by bombing, the water in the Floating Harbour could not drain into the river. It was shut permanently in 1952.

The basin gets its name from Charles Bragge Bathurst, an eminent Tory politician and supporter of the slave trade, who was an MP for Bristol from 1796–1811. He held several high offices of state, including Treasurer of the Royal Navy (like Samuel Pepys), Secretary at War, and Master of the Royal Mint (like Isaac Newton).

Close to the bridge are the lovely cast-iron balconies of the Louisiana Pub, formerly the Bathurst Hotel, dating from 1820. On the west side, facing the basin, is an attractive row of refurbished Regency houses from approximately the same date. The basin is also the home of the engine-less lightship "Lightvessel 55" built in Bristol by Charles Hill and Sons (see chapter 39) in 1886, now the headquarters of the Cabot Cruising Club and renamed *John Sebastian*.

Across the basin to the east, the imposing grand stone edifice with the octagonal corner tower is the former Bristol General Hospital, designed by W G Gyngell in the 1850s. It was substantially restored (it had lost the dome of the tower to a bomb in World War Two) and converted to private residences in 2017–18.

GAOL FERRY BRIDGE

GAOL FERRY BRIDGE

This lovely suspension bridge, with its pylons that echo the neo-gothic corner pinnacles on the tower of the nearby St Paul's church (1831 and 1958), was optimistically christened "Southville Bridge" by Alderman C P Billing when he opened it on 10th October 1935. However, the picaresque name which actually stuck was that of the ferry that preceded the bridge. "Gaol" ferry, in turn, was given its name from the close proximity of "New" Bristol Gaol, which opened its gates in 1820 and which dominated the north side of Cumberland Road a little distance to the east. This name came with gruesome associations that Alderman Billing no doubt was not keen to foreground. Notably, public hangings were carried out on the flat roof of the prison gateway. The gateway still exists, a few metres upstream of the bridge — a substantial stone arch flanked by a pair of squat towers. This is where four of the ringleaders of the infamous Bristol Riots of 1831 were hanged in front of a crowd of thousands. The last public hanging in the city took place here in 1849. Servant girl Sarah Harriet Thomas had bludgeoned to death her elderly employer, who had mistreated her. The girl had to be dragged screaming to the scaffold. She was 17-years-old. The gateway has now been lovingly restored and incorporated into the Wapping Wharf housing development. I trust that the residents sleep well.

Gaol ferry was established by Mr John Acraman in 1829, by agreement with the Bristol Dock Company. The Acraman family were significant figures in shipbuilding and ironfounding at this time in Bristol. The ferry fee to cross was a halfpenny per passenger and it soon became very busy and successful. The City Corporation took it over in 1854 and operated it until it closed with the completion of the new bridge, at which point it was being used by 10,000 people every month. Silting up of the New Cut meant that the ferryboat had become difficult to operate at very low tides, thus *"inconveniencing the working classes"* according to a local Labour councillor. The corporation decided to replace it with a bridge, built in 1934–5 above the old ferry slipways, for the sum of £2,600. It was made by the firm of David Rowell of Westminster, London. They had recently designed the Sparke Evans Park Bridge (chapter 12) in a similar style. It was installed by the City Engineers department. By the mid–1930s, masted packet boats operating regular services to Cardiff and Swansea from the Bathurst Basin were no longer navigating the New Cut, so the extra expense and complications of a lifting/swinging bridge were no longer necessary.

The original ferry slipway, on the south bank, is still there beneath the bridge. It is accessible with a little care.

Gaol Ferry Bridge is one of the few bridges in the world that has its own Twitter account (@gaolferrybridge).

VAUXHALL BRIDGE

Long, low and tapering elegantly, this lattice–work steel swing bridge is surprisingly streamlined for its date. It was opened with a silver key by the Lady Mayoress of Bristol on June 1st 1900. The total length is 82m and it cost £10,000. It was built to link the developing suburbs of Ashton and Southville with the rest of the city. The superstructure is one of several bridges built in Bristol by John Lysaght and Co. The foundations and masonry were by Messrs J Durnford and Son and the hydraulic machinery was made by Armstrong Whitworth and Co. The south abutment is of local Pennant sandstone, with red Devonian "Wilderness" sandstone quoins, caps and string courses. This came from the Wilderness Quarry at Micheldean, Gloucestershire. The Wilderness Quarry, which is now sadly closed, like several other famous stone quarries in Britain, received considerable attention from the geological community in Victorian times, when spectacular fossils were discovered during quarrying operations. In recent years it has provided this stone for Toronto City Hall (1965) and for the striking red banding in the facade of Sir James Stirling's masterpiece "No 1 Poultry" in the City of London (incorrectly referred to on some websites as pink limestone).

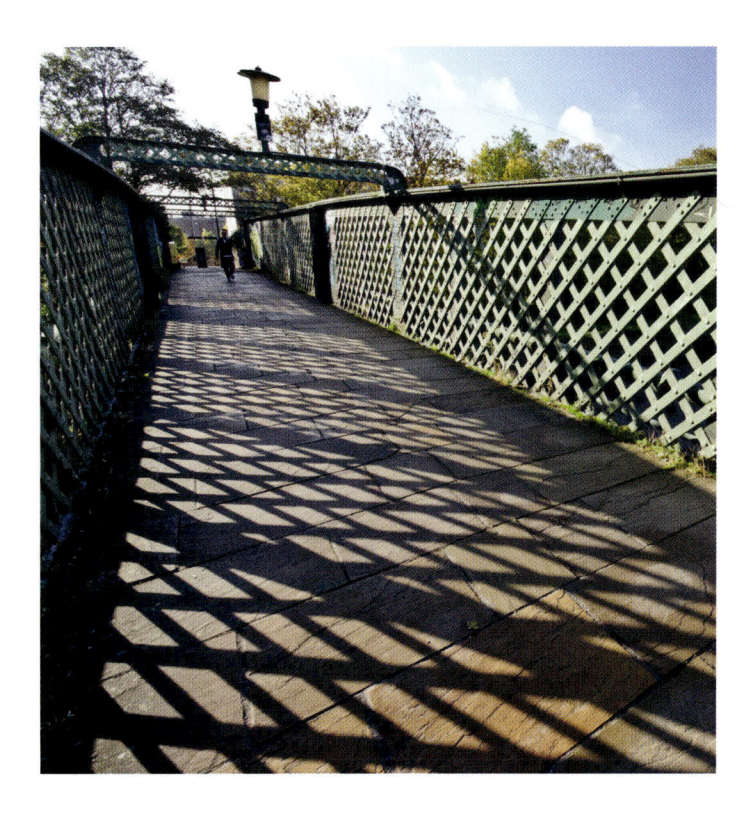

The swinging part of the bridge pivots on the adjacent square pier near the south bank, faced with Pennant and Chepstow stone surmounted by granite. This carries a steel drum housing the mechanism. At the base of this pier are "cutwaters" separated by an arch. On the north side, a smaller pier supports a fixed span over the towpath (called the "chocolate path" — the reason being obvious when you see it). Steel staircases descend to the towpath and to Cumberland Road. The walkway extension over Cumberland Road is a fairly recent addition. The swinging section is 158 ft long and weighs 150 tonnes. It allowed masted vessels to pass, which would enter the Floating Harbour via Bathurst Basin lock. When required to swing, a hydraulic mechanism lifted the swing part a few inches so that its upward-facing rollers made contact with an inverted roller path inside the drum. Hydraulic water power, to move the bridge, came from pumping engines in the nearby Underfall Yard at the west end of the Floating Harbour via a piping system which supplied the whole Port of Bristol with high pressure water power for cranes and moving bridges. River traffic which required the bridge to open declined in the 1920s, and the last swing was in 1935.

The new bridge put an end to the Vauxhall ferry which began operations near here in the 1860s. Until 1894, the ferry was located about 100m further downstream, very close to the Underfall Yard sluices on the north bank of the river. These controlled the level of water in the Floating Harbour by allowing excess water to be released. On 19th June 1894, the ferry with 10–20 people on board had just set off from the north bank when the sluice gates were opened, creating a wall of turbulent water. Some passengers seeing this panicked, and five of them tried to jump back onto the bank. The boat lurched, tipping all the rest of the passengers into the water. Two were drowned. The ferry was subsequently moved further upstream, closer to the location of the present bridge.

The ferry and bridge both took their name from the nearby Vauxhall shipyard on the Bedminster side opposite the Underfall Yard. It opened in 1840 as Acraman Morgan and Co, and passed to John Payne &Co in 1862. Many vessels were launched from there until it closed in 1925.

ASHTON AVENUE BRIDGE

Sadly, the bridge we see today is literally only half of what it used to be. Completed in 1906, it was of very unusual design — a "double decker" swing bridge. The upper level was a road for pedestrians and vehicles and the lower level carried the first railway line, very belatedly, into the north bank of the Floating Harbour, terminating at Canon's Marsh. The Great Western Railway Company (GWR) had long been reluctant to do this, but after much pressure eventually agreed, investing around £400,000 in the project with the proviso that the city council

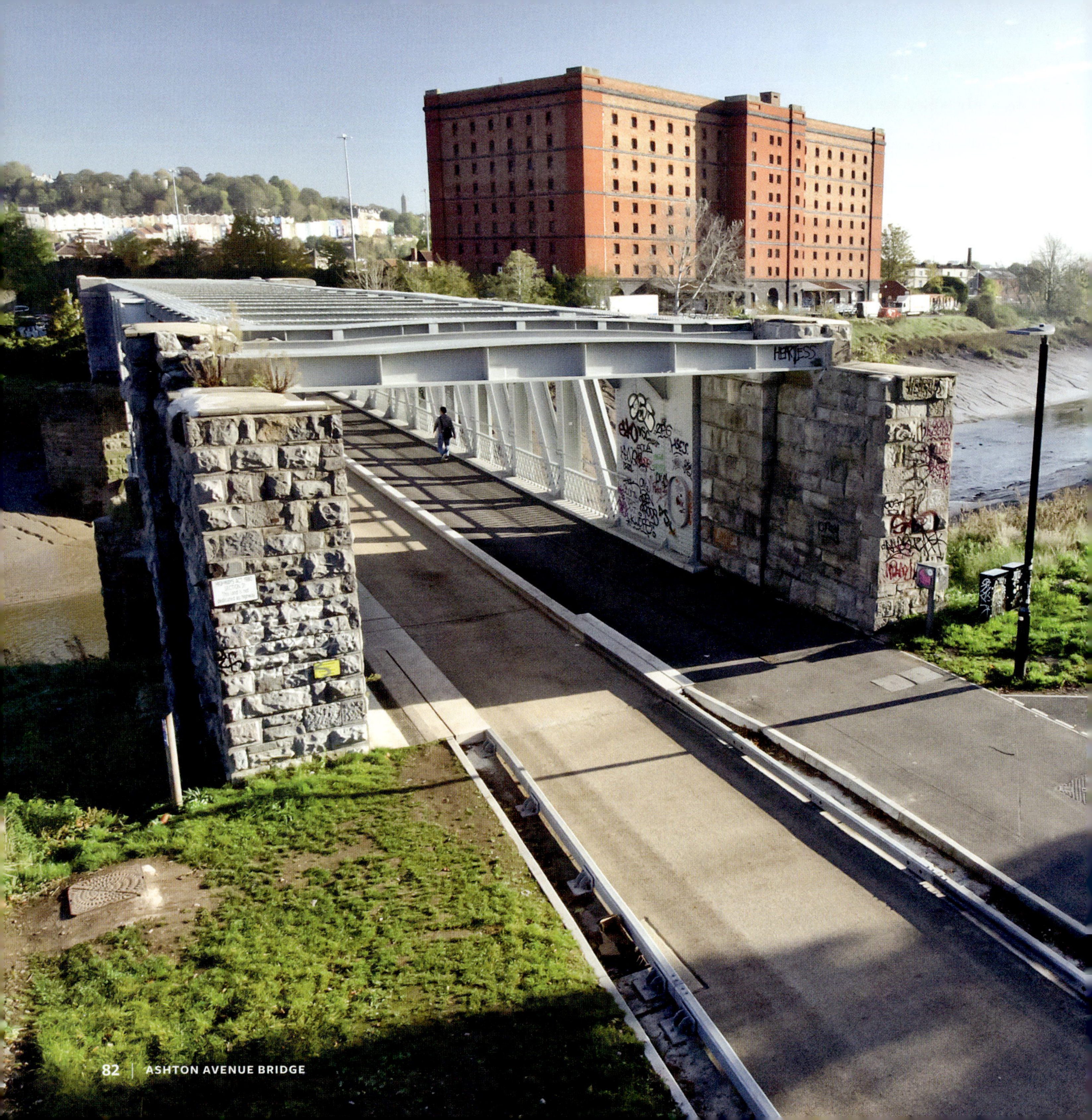

paid half of the costs of the new bridge, estimated at £36,000. Eventually, the bridge costs rose to twice that amount, with the GWR only contributing an extra £4,000.

It opened to much fanfare and acclaim, meriting a technical article in the January 1906 edition of the professional journal "The Engineer". If the rail approach spans were included, the bridge was over 180m long in total. One thousand and five hundred tonnes of steel were used, of which the swinging section, turned by hydraulics, weighs 1,000 tonnes. The roadway was 6m wide with two footpaths either side, each 1.6 m wide. The swinging section was 61m long and could turn up or downstream. There was a short fixed section extending from the north bank. The control cabin was prominently positioned high above the centre of the swinging span on an arched gantry. There was a complex system of interlocking between the movement of the bridge and the railway signals on each bank. The superstructure was made by the Bristol firm of John Lysaght and Co. The foundations were installed by Edmund Nuttall Ltd of Manchester. Hydraulic water power came from pumps in the nearby Underfall Yard in the Foating Harbour. Four new roads had to be constructed to give access to the upper roadway, with a fairly steep gradient. The bridge was a critical part of new comprehensive industrial development on the north side of the New Cut and Floating Harbour, particularly Canons Marsh. This included construction, between 1905 and 1919, of the giant redbrick bonded warehouses, the "Tobacco Bonds", for the storage of the wares of the Imperial Tobacco Company, one of which stands right next to the bridge. But the new bridge also had a significant impact on Bristolians' leisure pursuits. The management of the Bristol Tramways Company were delighted that it would open up *"new country"* for *"circular cab and carriage drives"* from Clifton and the city centre. At the opening ceremony, in which the Lady Mayoress opened the gates to the bridge, the Lord Mayor grandiloquently ventured that *"the possibility of vehicular communication [between Ashton Gate and Hotwells] would minister to the pleasure and satisfaction of the inhabitants"*.

After it opened, there was rapid development on the Somerset side. In 1907–8, the bridge swung open 3,401 times. In 1909, it was reported as having an "enormous traffic" over it. However, the next 30 years saw a dramatic drop in commercial river traffic using the Floating Harbour, and the bridge swung open for the last time in 1934.

When the nearby Plimsoll and Avon bridges opened in 1965 (chapters 32 and 35), the bridge became redundant for road traffic. The upper roadway was entrely removed and the railway line closed two years later. The bridge was given over to pedestrians and cyclists and, over the next 50 years, it became a neglected and dilapidated eyesore. But, in 2017, it rose up like a Phoenix from the ashes. It was substantially renovated and refurbished to carry the new Bristol Rapid Transit Bus System. Now, once again looking splendidly tough and muscular, it has recovered some of its former glory, and we can be sure that it will *"minister to the pleasure and satisfaction of the inhabitants"* for many more years in its new role.

AVON BRIDGE

Avon Bridge is joined by a short stretch of elevated roadway at its north end to the Plimsoll Bridge (chapter 35), and together they carry traffic north–south at high level across the eastern end of the New Cut, the east end of Spike Island (not really an island), and the entrance to the Floating Harbour. The bridges form part of the Cumberland Basin Gyratory System, which took two years to build and was completed in 1965. Eighteen businesses had to move and almost 60 homes had to be demolished to make way for it. It was Bristol's first multi-level traffic interchange. Before this new system was built, traffic had to cross the New Cut on the upper level of the Ashton Avenue swing bridge, and would then then cross the Floating Harbour over the bridges of the Junction Locks. But in the 1950s, long before the M4 and M5 existed, this had become a serious bottleneck to road traffic passing through Bristol. The North Junction Lock swing bridge was being opened 10 times a day and this often resulted in traffic jams several miles long.

The new "gyratory" was opened fully on April 14th 1965, at 12.30 am precisely, by Transport Minister Mr Tom Fraser. Despite heavy rain, scores of pedestrians were the first to cross the bridges accompanied by the sound of ships' sirens echoing down the Avon Gorge. But the Minister ominously warned Bristolians that he was "...*considering a congestion tax to beat city jams*... [*and was*]... *planning further steps to discourage people from using cars in and around city centres*... *Parking controls would have to be used more strongly in the future*". Aren't we fortunate that, 60 years later, we've got all that sorted out now?

Once the new route was opened, the Ashton Avenue Bridge was closed to all but pedestrians and cyclists and the approach roads removed (chapter 31).

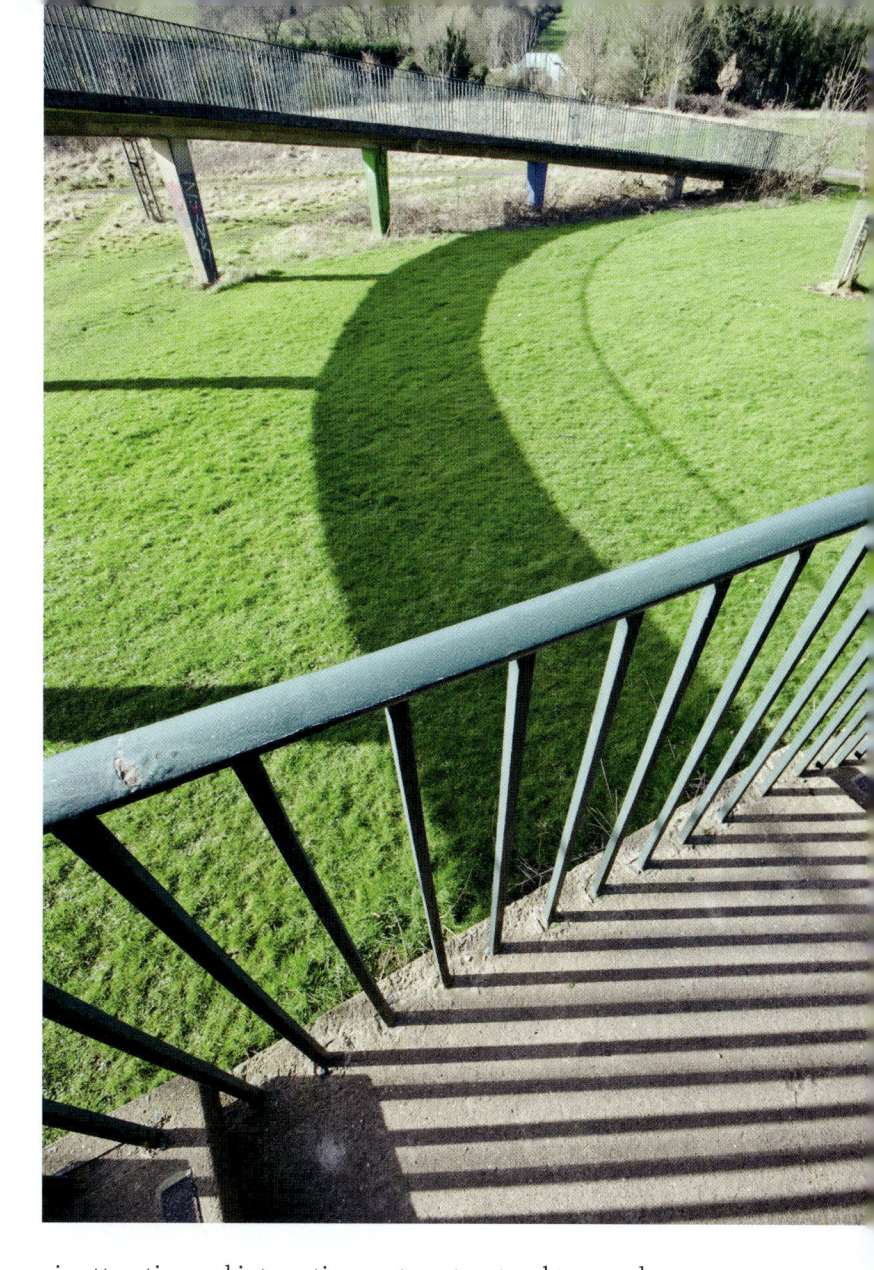

Avon Bridge, unlike the Plimsoll Bridge, does not swing — tall ships no longer sailed up the New Cut in 1965. It is a very plain pre-stressed concrete box structure of three spans, 70m long in total. The two central fin-like piers sit in the river, topped by shallow concrete arches. Although, at busy times, the traffic over the bridge can make it a rather hostile place for the walker, there are splendid views to be had from it of Clifton, Hotwells, the Avon Gorge and Cumberland Basin. However, it is not just the distant views that are of primary interest here, but the landscape and paths in, around, and importantly, *underneath* this complex of bridges and roads, which were designed by eminent landscape designer Sylvia Crowe (1901–77). She was a pioneering influence in the profession, and became President of the Landscape Institute. This scheme is of national significance as it is her most complete built road project, and she designed it in her sixties at the height of her powers. She took great care to design-in distant views, screening, segregation of pedestrians via attractive and interesting routes, structural tree and shrub planting, and integrated family amenities. There are subtle changes in ground height and slopes to achieve some of these aims and to trick the eye into thinking the whole was more than the sum of its parts. Although some of her scheme has been lost over time, particularly on the north bank of Cumberland Basin (see chapter 35), it is well worth

descending one of the several staircases that lead down from the elevated roadway to ground level and have a wander around. I particularly recommend the one on the south-west side of Avon Bridge that takes you down to a grassy area. A forest of stout piers holds up the gracefully curving and cambered roadway above you to form a sheltered space within the park. The underside of the approach roads on both banks was deliberately engineered to be a smooth, plain surface interrupted only by the support columns, although this effect has now been marred by the surface fixing of drainpipes in some places. There is a striking "constructivist" style to the spiral concrete staircases accessing the road which add focal points of interest. More information about the landscaping can be found on the "Parks and Gardens UK" website, and it is one of the walks in the book "Bristol Explored" by Tim Mowl.

The end may be approaching, however, for the entire Cumberland Basin Gyratory. In late 2017, the Mayor of Bristol, Marvin Rees, announced that he was putting together a proposal to remove this "old ugly road network across the western end of the harbour". Plimsoll Bridge will go, replaced by a new bridge further downstream, thus releasing land on Spike Island and both sides of the Avon for much-needed housing.

SOUTH ENTRANCE LOCK BRIDGE

William Jessop built two entrance locks, North and South, in close proximity for his Floating Harbour Scheme of 1804–9, to allow ships to enter Cumberland Basin and the Floating Harbour from the River Avon. Each was spanned by a hand-operated wooden swing bridge. But within a couple of decades, both locks were too narrow for the wider ships that had come into service. In 1844, the by now eminent engineer Isambard Kingdom Brunel was asked to design a new, wider, South Entrance Lock with an iron swing bridge, to be sited a few metres south of the original one. These works were completed in 1849, and most of Jessop's South Entrance Lock was filled in. Brunel's swing bridge was hand operated to begin with, but was converted to hydraulic water power when this became available in the docks in 1870. Brunel's Lock is the South Entrance Lock we see today, but in 1873 his swing bridge was shortened and moved to the North Entrance Lock when the latter was widened by Jessop's successor, Thomas Howard. Here it remained until the Plimsoll Bridge rendered it redundant in 1965. It was then placed on the lockside next to Howard's North Lock in the shadow of the Plimsoll Bridge.

The bridge over the South Entrance Lock that we now cross, installed in 1873 when Brunel's bridge was moved, is dubbed the "Replica Bridge". It was built by Edward Finch and Co of Chepstow as an exact copy of Brunel's. Look carefully at the unusual tubular girders on each side, made of wrought iron plates. This novel design was a milestone in Brunel's career — he subsequently scaled it up as the basis for the huge Royal Albert Bridge at Saltash, near Plymouth.

The South Entrance Lock was hardly used once Howard's larger North Lock was built. In 1894, a steamer landing stage was constructed on the River Avon side, rendering it unusable. More recently, access on the water from Cumberland Basin by anything larger than a rowing boat has been blocked by a concrete walkway resting on timber piers, which protects the Plimsoll Bridge when the latter is swung open (chapter 34).

SOUTH ENTRANCE LOCK WALKWAY

SOUTH ENTRANCE LOCK WALKWAY

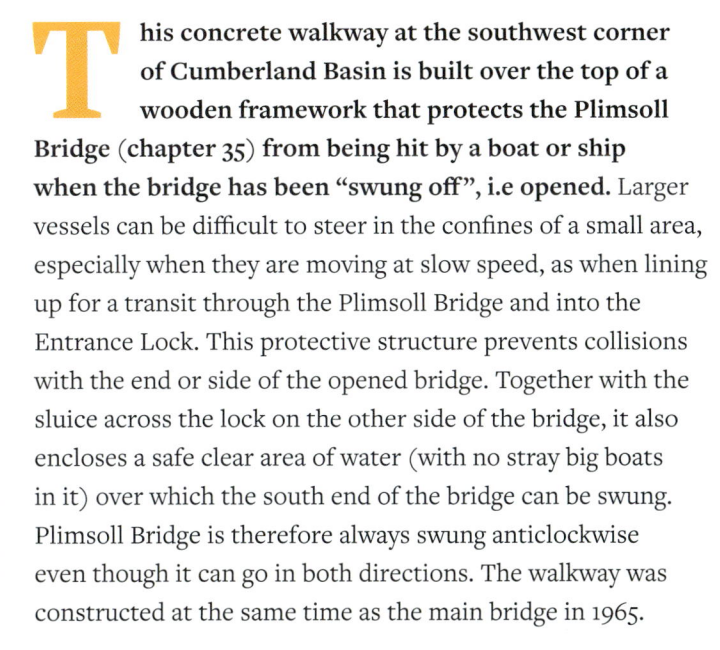

This concrete walkway at the southwest corner of Cumberland Basin is built over the top of a wooden framework that protects the Plimsoll Bridge (chapter 35) from being hit by a boat or ship when the bridge has been "swung off", i.e opened. Larger vessels can be difficult to steer in the confines of a small area, especially when they are moving at slow speed, as when lining up for a transit through the Plimsoll Bridge and into the Entrance Lock. This protective structure prevents collisions with the end or side of the opened bridge. Together with the sluice across the lock on the other side of the bridge, it also encloses a safe clear area of water (with no stray big boats in it) over which the south end of the bridge can be swung. Plimsoll Bridge is therefore always swung anticlockwise even though it can go in both directions. The walkway was constructed at the same time as the main bridge in 1965.

PLIMSOLL BRIDGE

Plimsoll Bridge, completed in 1965, is a steel swing bridge which is joined to Avon Bridge at its south end by a short section of roadway to form a single flyover. This forms the key part of the Cumberland Basin Gyratory System (see chapter 32) that connects the busy A3029 dual carriageway on the south side with the A4 on the north side. It is 82m long and weighs 865 tonnes. It was designed by the City Engineers in consultation with engineers Freeman Fox & Partners. The main contractor was Sir Robert McAlpine and Sons (South Wales) Ltd. The bridge machinery was made by Sir William Arrol and Co Ltd and the bridge superstructure was made by Head Wrightson

Teesdale Ltd. It is a twin box girder construction of stiffened plate, most of it not quite 1cm thick. A deck of steel plate sits on a pair of elegant gull-wing arms which are cantilevered from a central cross-girder. The central pivot rests on a concrete foundation, underneath which is a set of concrete piles sunk 20m into the riverbed, each 1m in diameter. Contrary to a prevalent urban myth, the bridge rotates *not* on a bed of mercury, but on a circular "race" of ball bearings. It is driven by two 22Kw motors acting through four drive pinions. The control tower is above the deck, on top of a 12m column giving a 360 degree view of the surroundings.

It takes about 40 seconds to open the bridge and it is an impressive sight. (You can find out the swing times from the Harbourmaster's Office.) The motion of this huge and heavy piece of metal is unexpectedly silent. It has occasionally stuck open, and the result, inevitably, is gridlock in the city centre. The first time it stuck was just 3.5 hours after the opening ceremony, and it caused the biggest traffic jam Bristol had ever known up to that date. It also stuck open in June 1976 during the hottest heatwave in Britain in the last century. Firefighters had to hose it down for four hours before it would close.

It is difficult to believe that the bleak area underneath the bridge approaches on the north bank of Cumberland Basin used to be the highlight of the landscaping in and around the interchange, carried out by eminent landscape architect Sylvia Crowe (see chapter 32). Here was "Cumberland Piazza", which accounted for 50 percent of the whole landscaping budget. It had a spiral fountain and paddling pool, a nautical themed playground, a cafe, seating and mature tree planting. Initially well used, the growth of traffic volume, noise, and concerns about pollution, together with lack of maintenance, meant that it was eventually abandoned and closed by the city council in the 1970s. The local community association has campaigned for years to reinvigorate it, but an announcement by the Mayor of Bristol to move the whole interchange further downstream, to make room for housing, may render this idea redundant.

Crossing over the Plimsoll Bridge gives splendid views to the west of the Avon Gorge, the Clifton Suspension Bridge and the entrance locks of the Floating Harbour, and to the east, Cumberland Basin and the three huge redbrick Tobacco Bond warehouses. The basin was made large enough to allow many tall-masted sailing ships to wait here for a few hours until the tide had risen enough to allow them to proceed out through the locks into the river and away. When the basin was full of ships it must have been quite a sight.

The bridge is named after famous Bristolian Samuel Plimsoll (1824–98), who was born at 9 Colston Parade, Redcliffe. There is a statue of him on Capricorn Quay, opposite the SS Great Britain. He became a Liberal politician (MP for Derby) and social reformer, keenly interested in safety at sea. He is best known for his campaign that led to the Merchant Shipping Act of 1876 that required, amongst

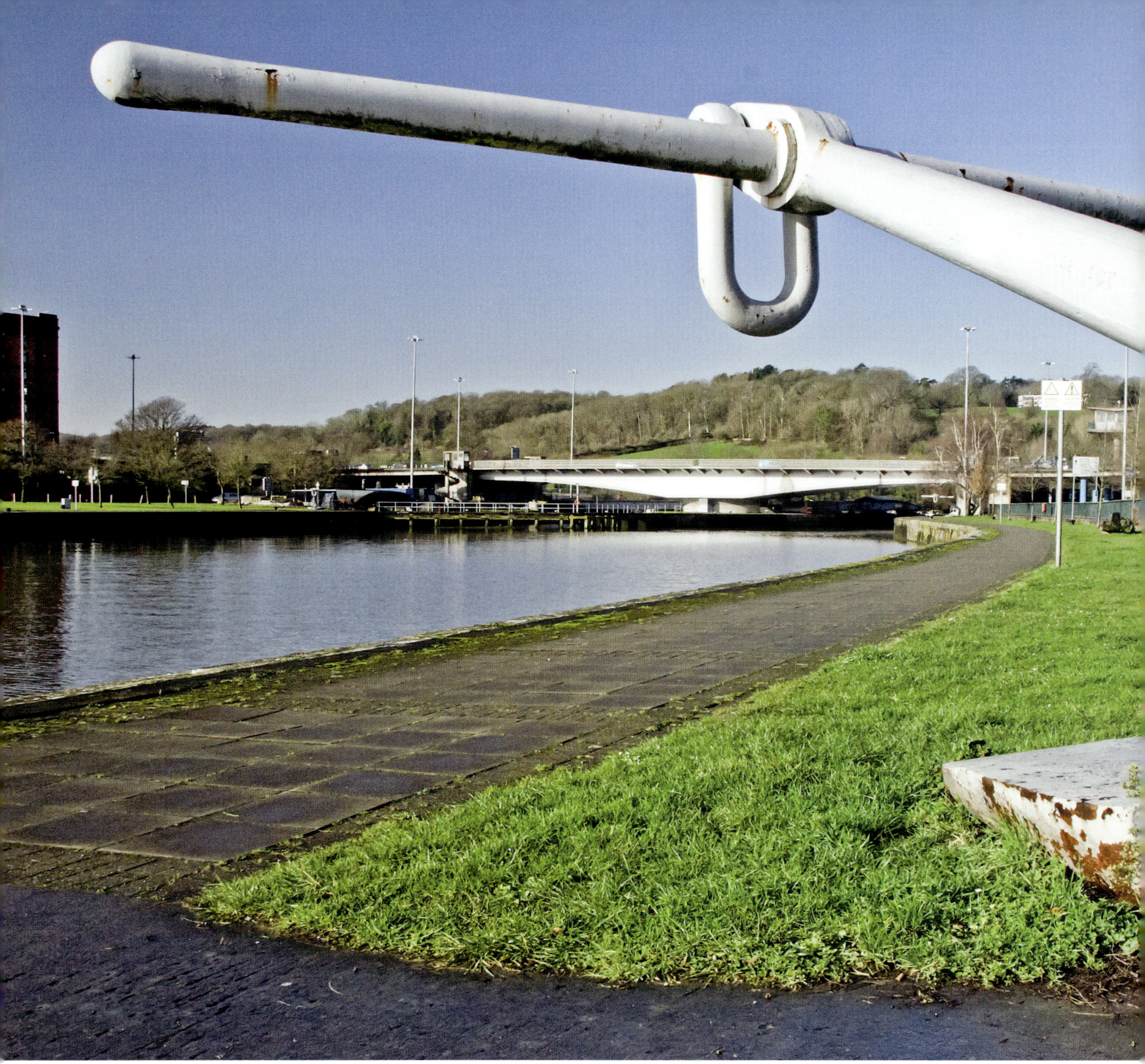

other reforms, the now famous 'Plimsoll Line' to be painted on the hull of every ship to show when it has been loaded to its maximum safe capacity. Plimsoll would probably have been amused that "plimsoll" gym shoes were also indirectly named after him. The rubber sole of the plimsoll, unlike trainers, is not "lipped" up the canvas sides of the shoe. The effect when running is supposedly like running without shoes — hence their popularity. They were developed as beachwear in the 1830s by the Liverpool Rubber Company. Originally called a "sand shoe", they acquired the nickname "plimsoll" in the 1870s, probably (no one is certain) because the coloured horizontal band joining the upper to the sole resembled the Plimsoll Line on a ship's hull and/or because, just like the Plimsoll Line on a ship, if water gets above the line of the rubber sole, your feet get wet!

Plimsoll Bridge had a design life of 20 years. It has clocked up well over three times that amount, but it may not see many more if the Mayor's aforementioned plans are realised.

CLIFTON SUSPENSION BRIDGE

Bristol is very lucky to have this remarkable, beautiful and historic filigree necklace of iron draped across its shoulders. And at night, when the lights are on, the iron necklace turns into one made of diamonds! Few cities in the world have such a structure in a dramatic setting like the Avon Gorge, so close to the city centre.

The Latin inscription at the top of the towers, *Suspensa Vix Via Fit*, is a play on the name of the initial benefactor and means "a suspended way built with difficulty". The story of the Clifton Suspension Bridge is, indeed, a long tale of vexations, and in the space I have here I can only give an outline. The curious can find out more at the bridge's adjacent Visitor Centre (free entry, open every day).

The story begins in 1754 with the death of a self-made Bristol wine merchant William Vick. In his Will, he left £1,000 to the city's Society of Merchant Venturers, Bristol's ancient society of businessmen and financiers. This sum was to be invested until it reached £10,000, at which point it was to be used to build a bridge over the highest, narrowest point in the Avon Gorge. Vick thought that this would be "*of great publick utility*", the reason being that, at the time of his death, the only river crossing in Bristol was Bristol Bridge, then a 500-year-old mediaeval timber structure that was narrow and crowded. A bridge spanning the gorge would be high enough for tall ships to pass beneath — essential for the busy port that Bristol was at that time.

By 1829, Vick's fund stood at £8,000, the equivalent of about £500,000 today. The Bristol Chamber of Commerce were pressing for a steamship port to be set up at Portishead which would need a good road link to the centre of Bristol, crossing the Avon. The Merchant Venturers therefore felt the time had come for the new bridge. They formed a Trust to raise more money and to build the bridge. Unfortunately, the Bridge Trustees were so determined to create something with the "wow!" factor that would help to put Bristol on the map that they largely overlooked the shaky business case behind the venture. A chronic lack of funding, poor management and some bad luck made the construction of the bridge an extremely long, drawn out "stop-go" process. It took 28 years to complete the bridge, by which time the "*reckless engineer*", as someone once called its designer, had died.

The Trustees held a competition in 1829 for the design of the new bridge, specifying that it should be of a suspension type. Many entries were submitted. Among them were four designs by an unknown 23-year-old of limited experience by the name of Isambard Kingdom Brunel. The competition was judged by the 70-year-old Thomas Telford, regarded as the father of British engineering. Telford's own new Menai Suspension Bridge (1826) in North Wales then held the world record for longest single span, 176m. At Clifton, the length required was over 200m. This had never before been attempted by a single span, as Brunel and some other entrants were proposing. Telford was understandably cautious and did not regard any of the submitted designs as satisfactory and/or having enough safety margin. The committee asked Telford to submit his own design, which he did, to the approbation of the committee. But the general public hated it and it was costly. The committee rapidly backtracked and announced a second competition, this time to be judged by two eminent men, a mathematician and a scientist. Brunel resubmitted three of his earlier designs with small modifications, plus a new fourth which, was a sop to Telford's criticisms. The design by Smith and Hawkes was announced the winner. Brunel immediately went to see the judges and had discussions. Brunel was then announced the winner instead, with one of his single span designs. In public, Smith and Hawkes were graceful. Their private reaction is not known, which is probably just as well.

The cost was estimated at £52,000. Brunel noted in his diary "...*I anticipate a pleasant job, for the expense seems no object provided it is made grand.*" Vick's legacy was wholly inadequate, so funds had to be raised from loans and donations. The tolls to be charged would provide the interest on the loans. The prospectus for the bridge invited investment in "...*a monument to architectural taste and splendour without parallel...*". The well–heeled citizens of Bristol were somewhat cautious — it took over a year to raise £32,000, mostly as loans. With a shortfall of about £15,000, and aware of the risk, the Bridge Committee went ahead with the expectation that the rest of the money would be raised when the public saw the bridge underway. On 21st June 1831, a low-key ceremony was held to mark the start of the project. In his speech, a local dignitary promised that the bridge would be "...*a stupendous work, the ornament of Bristol and the wonder of the age.*" Brunel was later to refer to the bridge as "...*my first child, my darling...*". The local press were confident the bridge would be a financial success. In October, four months later, came the first inkling of future problems — funds were still not adequate. Then, on October 29th, came a disaster. The Bristol Reform Law Riots were sparked off by the failure of Bristol's senior magistrate, and MP for Boroughbridge, to support the Parliamentary Reform Bill which would have corrected injustices and anomolies in the Parliamentary system and widened the franchise. The riots in Bristol were the bloodiest and most costly of any that occurred in Britain in the 19th century. Between 10 and 150 (estimates vary widely) people were killed and the economic damage was huge. Confidence in the city took a nose-dive, and without a stone having been laid, the bridge project was halted.

It took five years for boldness of spirit to return to prompt a re-start. More money was raised, though still leaving a considerable shortfall. The foundation stone of the Leigh Woods abutment was laid on 27th August 1836, in grand style before a crowd of some 60,000 people, by the President of the British Association for the Advancement of Science. This was preceded by a procession of 400 city dignitaries, headed by the Association President. Brunel walked in second place, in isolation, behind the President's carriage, followed by everybody else. Brunel was not one to shun the limelight.

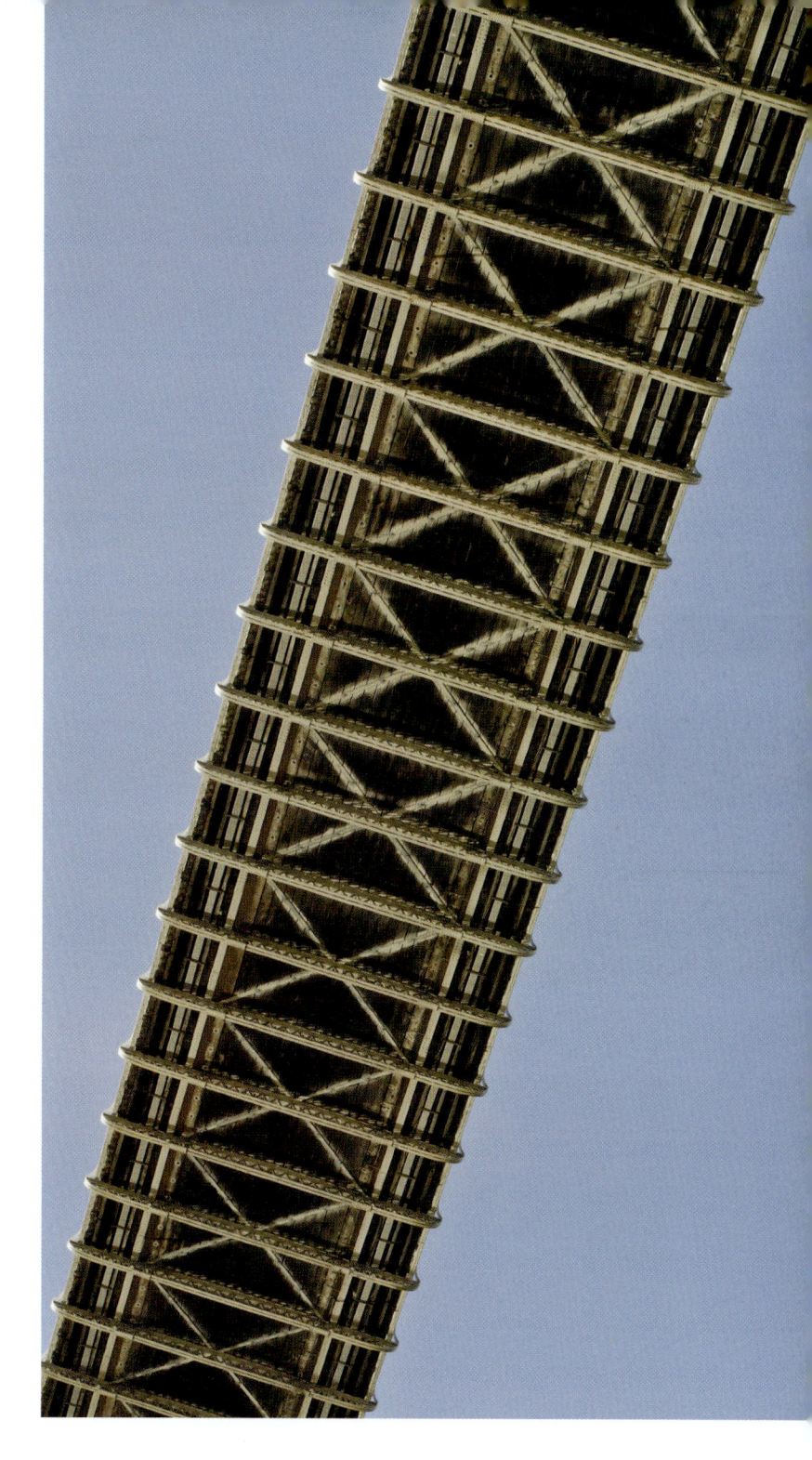

Work on the bridge proceeded excrutiatingly slowly. In 1843, after seven years, the towers, abutments and the approach roads were finished but all the money was gone and work stopped once more. The project had been grossly mismanaged, by both the Trustees and Brunel himself. In 1851, Brunel was instructed to sell the ironwork that had been purchased and, in 1853, the land on which the bridge stood reverted back to the original donors, the Merchant Venturers. In 1859, Brunel suffered a stroke, and died six days later. He never saw his "darling" completed. The bare towers were seen as an eyesore. The Clifton Improvement Society called them "Vicks folly" and wanted them demolished.

In 1860, the Institute of Civil Engineers came to the rescue and took the initiative to get the bridge finished "... *as a fitting monument to... [Brunel]... and to remove a slur from the engineering talent of the country*". They were prompted by the availability of a set of second-hand suspension chains from the dismantling of Hungerford footbridge in London — also by Brunel. Engineers Hawkshaw and Barlow came up with cost-saving and other proposals that made significant changes to the engineering design. But an additional £45,000 was needed. A limited company was formed, and this time the full amount was raised without difficulty by a share issue and loans. Work started again in late 1862 and, just two years later, the finally finished bridge was tested with 500 tonnes of stone placed on it (was this task an optional one for the workmen I wonder?).

The opening ceremony was on 8th December 1864, at which an estimated 160,000 people thronged the Clifton Downs and Cumberland Basin. There was a one-mile long procession from the city centre that included 16 bands. There were church bells, there were flags, there was a six-gun salute. The two Lords-Lieutenant of Somerset and Gloucester formally opened the bridge. There was a banquet for the dignitaries, beer and sandwiches for the workmen. No member of the Brunel family attended. The modifications made to the bridge by Hawkshaw and Barlow meant that the bridge was no longer "pure" Brunel, and the family felt that the ceremony did not sufficiently honour him.

Over the course of the next 100 years, the Clifton Suspension Bridge Trust gradually bought out the private shareholders, so that the bridge is now wholly owned by a Charitable Trust. For the first 80 years, the toll income provided a poor return to the investors. It was only after the 1920s, as car ownership spread, that toll income achieved respectable figures. Vehicle crossings are now approximately 3,000,000 per year and the bridge operates without any public subsidy.

The bridge is a Grade I Listed structure. The weight of the ironwork is 1,500 tonnes. The chains contain a total of 4,200 links, each of 0.5 tonnes. Considering its exposed position, the bridge structure has shown remarkable little corrosion — it still has 99 percent of its original wrought ironwork and is the only early suspension bridge that survives in substantially unaltered and unstrengthened state. The Bridge Master is a fully qualified engineer who manages a team of 13 bridge attendants and one maintenence employee, who carry out a programme of rigorous monitoring of the the bridge and regular maintenence work, supported by consultant engineers. Work on the bridge from underneath is carried out from a cradle that travels under the deck.

Had the bridge been completed on the date originally planned, it would, for a while, have been the longest (214m between piers) and highest (76m deck to water) suspension bridge in the world.

AVONMOUTH ROAD BRIDGE

The megastructure we call the Avonmouth Roadbridge was completed in 1974 as part of the gradual extension southwards of the M5 from Birmingham to Exeter. It was designed by Freeman Fox and Partners. The main contractor was the then Chepstow–based engineers Fairfield–Mabey. Tarmac Civil Engineering (which became the ill–fated Carillion) built the foundations and concrete piers.

The bridge was a small part of the plan, begun in 1962, to build 1,000 miles of motorway network throughout the UK by the early 1970s. The chair of the local county Highways Committee hoped that it would make Bristol "...*the London*

102 | AVONMOUTH ROAD BRIDGE

of the West". It was also needed to relieve the serious traffic congestion that happened every summer in Bristol when holiday traffic from the north, that was bound for the West Country on the A38, headed through the city centre.

The initial cost was £4.2m. The main bridge span across the water is 174m long and 40m wide but the overall length including the approach gradients is 1,387m. It rises 30.5m above the river to allow coastal shipping to pass underneath — although by the time it opened, the volume of such shipping going up the Avon to Bristol was just a trickle, so to speak. The height also helps to reduce noise and air pollution.

The method of construction was essentially quite simple. Huge hollow steel boxes, each 6m wide x 3m high x 18m long, were fabricated at ground level. Each weighed around 80 tonnes. They were then lifted up into position by crane and welded together end to end, one by one, to make a continuous "box girder". Two parallel "box girders", in line with the road, rest on paired concrete columns and a flat road deck was placed on top. Construction proceeded towards the water from each bank — meeting in the middle. Fairfield–Mabey engineers designed and built two novel "hover-platforms" from standard industrial parts, incorporating corrugated iron and stiff plastic sheet, to move them around over the soft ground at the site before they were lifted into position. The total weight of steelwork in the bridge is 13,000 tonnes. Roughly 130,000 vehicles a day cross this bridge.

Construction began in 1969 with a view to completion in 1972. Eight houses had to be demolished, and compensation was paid to these and other homeowners deemed to be in the affected area. Houses very close to the bridge were provided with double/ triple glazing and some were fitted with air purifiers. Shortly after work began on the bridge the first problem occurred in what was to become a long history of misfortunes. Around 1969-70, a series of failures of box-girder bridges occurred around the world. A UK government committee of inquiry was rapidly convened and made recommendations which required a redesign of the bridge's steelwork. This, together with industrial disputes, delayed the opening by two years to 23rd May 1974. Geoff Booth, then a young graduate engineer who was part of the construction team, relates:

"On the morning of the opening I was on the bridge deck with a team of erectors tightening down the bolts to the last lot of the lighting columns. The police were standing by. We reported that we had finished. There was no ceremony — the police indicated that the large timber baulks diverting southbound M5 traffic along the Portway could be pulled clear. One of our teams quickly did that. I watched a police officer vigorously waving an unsuspecting motorist over the bridge — a Citroen... one of the larger ones. The driver was clearly confused... we suspected that he hadn't realised that he was the first to cross."

The absence of any opening ceremony probably indicates how desperate Bristolians were for this bridge to relieve the annual misery in the city centre. Did the first person to drive across it realise they were making history? If the Citroen driver is still alive and happens to read this, I would be delighted to hear from you!

The opening of the bridge put an end to the historic Pill–Shirehampton ferry which had been operating at least since the mediaeval period, perhaps earlier, first as a rowboat, and then, from 1935, as a motorboat.

In late 1999, the bridge was the scene of a tragic industrial accident. Four welders were working on a movable platform that ran on tracks underneath the bridge. The men were probably moving the platform when it came off the rails, leaving it suspended by a single point to the bridge. The four were tipped out and all were killed. The contractors (Costain and Kvaerner Cleveland Bridge) were subsequently each fined £500,000 plus £525,000 in costs for what the judge termed *"widespread failings of the most serious nature"*. A plaque commemorating the dead workmen is attached to one of the support pillars.

104 | AVONMOUTH ROAD BRIDGE

After 20 years of use, 1995 saw the beginning of five years of upgrading and remedial work on the bridge that cost £125m. The load-carrying capacity was increased, an extra carriageway on either side was added and general remedial work was carried out inside the box girders. Only one year after this work had finished, the discovery of water penetration into the road surface meant that lanes had to close again for a complete resurfacing. And just five years after that it became apparent that complete resurfacing was once again required. This was completed in 2009.

The upstream landscape here is of high quality, rural and picturesque. Downstream is now mostly tarmac, but 40 years ago there were still largely open fields down to the sea. If it were proposed today to plonk a gigantic motorway bridge here, you could expect considerable opposition from environmentalists and the local community. In fact, the only protests about the Avonmouth Bridge were concerned with getting it finished as quickly as possible to relieve the traffic congestion in the city.

The bridge may not be beautiful, but it is certainly sublime; that is, awe inspiring and slightly scary, and to really "get" this behemoth, you need to explore the gloomy, arid, vegetation-free rainshadow underneath it. If it's a weekday morning, Nicky's Nosh van will usually be parked in the vast, dramatic space where the bridge crosses the Portway to offer you refreshment (table and seats provided). If you visit in the early evening with the sun setting, you could easily imagine a performance of Wagners Ring Cycle taking place here, with the M5 standing in for the Rainbow Bridge. Though I must admit that Gordano Services is not quite on a par with Valhalla.

It is also well worth making an extra diversion (five mins) to the north riverbank where you are rewarded with fine views upstream to Pill and downstream to the sea (see Walk Instructions p138 for directions).

THE PORTWAY VIADUCT

If you have lived in Bristol for some time, you have probably crossed this bridge in your car a thousand times and not given it a second thought. From a speeding vehicle you are just about aware of some dingy plain parapets and assumed the rest of the bridge was just as plain and dingy. How wrong you are! This turns out to be one of Bristol's lovliest bridges, both in itself and for its setting.

This bridge was an integral part of the construction of the 8km long Portway Road completed in 1926 at a total cost of £800,000. When it was opened by the then Minister of Transport, it was the most expensive road per kilometre ever constructed in Britain. Eight hundred men had worked on it for five years. It was built primarily to facilitate freight transport to and from the newly expanding docks and suburb at Avonmouth.

It was designed and built by Bristol City Corporation, with hefty financial assistance from central government. The man in charge was the city's Chief Engineer, Mr Lessel S. McKenzie, who was reported as having *"...a keen eye for the picturesque"*. If you look back at the Viaduct from the Lower Trym Valley which it spans, you cannot but agree. The bridge, in its arcadian setting, really does look like a landscape by Constable. The corporation did seem to appreciate that the Portway would run through a unique and beautiful landscape and was prepared to spend money to make the roadway integrate well with its surroundings. Much careful tree planting was done, quality materials were chosen as appropriate to the surroundings, and the scars made during construction were all made good.

The bridge was only originally intended to have three arches, but because of weak ground it had to be extended to six. The basic structure is concrete, faced with limestone quarried close by at the Hotwells end of the road. The parapets, keystones and string course are of contrasting red "Corsehill" sandstone from Dumfries.

At the opening ceremony the City Fathers were clearly proud of their work. *"...in years to come [the Portway] would be thought to be a magnificent piece of work"* said the Lord Mayor. He was echoed by the chair of the Docks Committee: *"...anyone who paid rates or taxes walking along it would think it a very fine road indeed!"*.

We no longer lavish such praise on new roads, and we look wistfully at Georgian watercolour paintings of the Avon Gorge showing nothing but a few sheep munching away quietly near the water's edge. But perhaps we can be thankful that the Portway might have been far worse had it not been for Lessel S McKenzie's "eye for the picturesque".

POOLE'S WHARF BRIDGE

Although now permanently water-filled, Poole's Wharf Marina was originally a dry dock, half its present size, called the "Little Dock". It was part of the Hotwells Shipyard that played a very prominent role in the city's maritime history and economy for over 150 years.

The dock was built by William Champion in 1768. At the same time he also built a huge wet dock immediately to the west, "Champions Dock", and a second dry dock immediately to the east, larger than the Little Dock, called the "Great Dock". Rownham Mead housing estate now covers the area once occupied by Champions/Merchants Dock and Poole's Court housing now covers the area of the Great Dock.

In 1773, James Martin Hilhouse, aged just 23, set himself up as a shipbuilder and bought the two dry docks. He constructed three slipways immediately east of the Great Dock, roughly where the Poole's Court waterfront garden is today. He leased the Little Dock to another shipbuilding partnership, Noble, Champion and Farr. Hilhouse's Great Dock was about the same size as Poole's Wharf Marina is now (the latter, as the Little Dock, has been enlarged over time). Noble, Champion and Farr occupied the Little Dock for about 25 years, but the real story here is about James Hilhouse and his Great Dock and slipways.

Hilhouse inherited money from his father and grandfather, who had developed a successful shipping business. James' father also made money by financing "privateering", whereby the government licensed privately-owned armed ships to attack French and Spanish merchant ships in times of war and keep a portion of the spoils. James Hilhouse's shipbuilding company, and its successor, Charles Hill and Sons, became the most important shipbuilders in Bristol, building 560 ships over a 200-year period. The first was a merchant ship of 270 tonnes, the "Exeter", launched in 1773. Their first ship for the Royal Navy, who became significant clients, was a frigate called the Medea. It was launched in 1778, closely followed by the "Crescent" and the "Cleopatra". In the next eight years Hilhouse built a further nine warships for the Navy on his slipways, all of which were used to fight our upstart colonists in the American Revolutionary War (spoiler alert — we lost!). In 1785, Hilhouse launched the 1,406 tonne 64-gun "Nassau", the largest ship yet built in Bristol.

By 1820, the company was operating from a total of four shipyards in the harbour. They closed down their operations at the Hotwells shipyard in 1823. In 1845, the company became Charles Hill and Sons when shipwright Charles Hill acquired the firm. The company diversified and, in addition to building ships, Hill built up a shipping fleet of North American-built sailing ships, the "Blue Star" line for the West Indies trade. In 1879, Hill's son established the Bristol City Line (BCL), which carried cargoes between Bristol and New York. In 1881, the company built its first iron ship, and then moved into steel sailing vessels. They specialised mainly in commercial ships, but also built warships and government vessels, especially during the First and Second World Wars. By the time Hill's grandson died in 1900, the firm owned 10 steamships, including the "Bristol City", at the time the largest ship ever constructed in Bristol. BCL ceased operations in 1974 and Hills shipbuilders went out of business in 1977.

When Charles Hill moved out of the Hotwells yard, another shipbuilder and a coal merchant moved in. Stothert and Marten (which became G K Stothert and Son) took over the Little Dock (Poole's Wharf Marina) and Hilhouse's slipways. The Great Dock was filled in.

James Paul Poole, a coal merchant, moved in to the very easternmost end of the site, which then became known as Poole's Wharf. Poole lived nearby on Hotwells Road and became a successful grocer as well as a coal merchant. One of his seven sons, also called James, took over and grew the family business, becoming wealthy and influential in Bristol. He was the director of three railway companies, one-time chairman of the Bristol Docks committee and a magistrate. He became the Mayor of Bristol in 1858 and died in 1872. His home was Wick House in Brislington — a grand mansion still in existence (now a nursing home). One of his younger brothers, Paul Falconer Poole, became an acclaimed English artist, largely self-taught. He exhibited his first work in the Royal Academy at the age of 25 and was made an academician in 1861. His paintings are hung in many UK galleries including the Tate, Royal Academy, Victoria and Albert Museum, and Bristol City Art Gallery.

Although shipbuilding finished at Hotwells Shipyard in 1904, ship repair continued until the 1930s. Another coal merchant, Osborne and Wallis, took over the whole site in 1934. In 1970, it finally became the last base for Bristol's sand-dredging fleet (Sand Supplies (Western) Ltd), operating in the Bristol Channel. The sand brought here was used in the building industry. These operations closed in 1991 and redevelopment for housing began in this part of the harbour as one of the final parts of the long-term plan to turn the harbour from a redundant port into a leisure and pleasure destination. The former Hills Albion Dockyard, a few hundred yards east of Poole's Wharf Marina, on the opposite side of the harbour, was occupied by Abel's Shipbuilders in 1980. Abel's were the last shipbuilders in Bristol until they, too, closed in 2016 when the owner retired. Thus closed a major chapter in Bristol's history.

The attractive double-leaf swing footbridge which enables you to cross the entrance to Poole's Wharf Marina was built in 1999. Provision of the bridge at the developers expense was a condition of the planning consent obtained by Crest Homes for building the housing on the east side of the marina. A design concept drawing for it was prepared by Philip Thorpe, the in-house architect for Crest Homes. This was interpreted and realised by engineer Geoff Gudge of HLD Ltd in Gainsborough, who were contracted to detail the design and supply the bridge. The steelwork structure was fabricated by Goole Welding Ltd. Capita Symonds designed the concrete foundations. The total cost was £170,000.

The two leaves of the bridge were prefabricated and brought to Bristol by road. As the new houses around the marina were already inhabited, it was considered unwise to lift them into the site over the rooftops, so a large floating crane was hired to make this unnecessary. At the time, there was only one such suitable crane available in the UK, located in Scotland. It took two weeks' sailing to get to Bristol. When the crane arrived in the harbour, the bridge halves were delivered by lorry to the nearest accessible part of the harbourside. They were then transferred, one at a time, to a floating pontoon using a mobile crane on the dockside. The pontoon then ferried each bridge half to Poole's Wharf Marina, where the floating crane did its job in lifting the halves from the pontoon into their current position. The original lock gate at the entrance to the marina proved difficult to take away so it was given an aquatic burial by being simply pulled over by the floating crane. Originally arduously hand operated, the bridge is now opened by electric power.

NORTH JUNCTION LOCK BRIDGE

William Jessop's Floating Harbour scheme of 1804–9 provided a single "junction" lock between Cumberland Basin to the west and the Floating Harbour to the east. But by the middle years of the 19th century, Jessop's junction lock had become too narrow for many of the the larger ships then in service. A new junction lock, the one you cross now, was constructed immediately north of the original one by Jessop's successor as Docks Engineer, Thomas Howard. It opened for the first time in 1871. It had an iron bridge between the pair of lock gates. The current steel swing bridge dates from 1925 and replaced the original one. This bridge was built by John Lysaght & Co., at the time Bristol's major steelwork company. The lock itself is rarely closed now but it does have modern flood defence gates which are closed when the tide in the river is expected to rise higher than the harbour level. The original water–hydraulic turning mechanism was installed by Armstrong Whitworth of Newcastle upon Tyne. This has only recently (2010) been replaced with a modern hydraulic oil system. At the same time, the lifting and turning mechanism was replaced with an improved design that minimises stresses on the parts, leading to reduced maintenance and a long life.

For the first 50 years of the Floating Harbour, human (or animal) power, via capstans and treadmills, was used to open the locks and bridges and to work the cranes. But in 1870, with the rebuilt Cumberland Basin locks came a new technology — hydraulic water power. The elegant Italianate stone building with a squat tower on the quayside just northeast of North Junction Lock was the first hydraulic engine house (now the Pumphouse pub). It contained two 33Kw steam engines that generated hydraulic water pressure of 52 bars. This was conveyed to the opening machinery of the locks and swing bridges in steel pipework. It was superseded by the Underfall Pumping House (at the far eastern end of Cumberland Basin) in the late 1880s.

A small nearby curiosity is a polished white granite drinking fountain built into the stone wall flanking the southern end of Merchant's Road that leads to the bridge. It was probably installed around 1859 along with many other drinking fountains in Bristol. It is of a type used extensively throughout Britain by the Metropolitan Drinking Fountain & Cattle Trough Association. This was a philanthropic association set up in London by Samuel Gurney, a Member of Parliament, and Edward Thomas Wakefield, a barrister, in 1859, to provide free clean and uncontaminated drinking water to the general public at a time when that supplied by the water companies was often anything but, and could sometimes carry serious, even fatal, diseases.

SOUTH JUNCTION LOCK BRIDGE

SOUTH JUNCTION LOCK BRIDGE

This lock belongs to William Jessop's scheme of 1804-9, and is so-called because it is at the junction of Cumberland Basin to the west and the Floating Harbour to the east, and allowed passage between the two. It is the only remaining intact part of Jessop's original scheme. An engraving of the 1830s shows Junction Lock Bridge to have a single low arch. It would have had to swing open, was almost certainly wooden and of two halves.

By the middle years of the 19th century, the lock had become too narrow for many of the the larger ships then in service. A new, wider junction lock was built in 1871, about 50m to the north. Jessop's Junction Lock soon became disused. The lock gates were removed in the 1890's and replaced with a fixed sluice gate as we see today, effectively sealing the lock. At the same time, the swing bridge was removed and replaced with a fixed, wider bridge. The lock is now an attractive anchorage for small boats. On the north side of the lock is a terraced row of pretty cottages built by The Bristol Dock Company for dock workers in 1831. On the south side stands the attractive three storey Nova Scotia Hotel and Pub, built just a few years earlier. It was originally a terrace of three houses but was converted into a coaching inn.

Jessop's Junction Lock became woven into the story of the SS Great Britain when the latter was launched at the Albion Dock in the Floating Harbour in 1843. This ship, designed by Isambard Kingdom Brunel, was the first ocean-going ship to have an iron hull and a screw propeller, and when launched was the largest vessel afloat in the world. She originally carried 252 passengers and 130 officers and crew but, when an extra deck was added, it increased the number of passengers to 730. The launching, or more accurately, the 'floating out', took place on 19th July 1843, attended by HRH Prince Albert.

It had been agreed at an early stage with the Dock Company that the Entrance Lock, allowing the ship to exit Cumberland Basin into the River Avon, was going to need substantial modifications to get the ship through. What took everyone by surprise was the discovery, after the launch, that the ship was not going to be able to get through the preceeding Junction Lock either. It was expected that the sloping sides of the hull would oversail the walls of the lock, but the ship was sitting too low in the water on account of the weight of machinery that had been fitted into it. Junction Lock would have to be modified as well. The Dock Company prevaricated for over a year, citing the need for an Act of Parliament to give them authority for such modifications. It was only in October 1844, after the Board of Trade intervened, that the Dock Company put the modifications in hand and at last, in December, the SS Great Britain successfully passed through Junction Lock into Cumberland Basin. But the main drama was yet to come. As the ship made its way through the Entrance Lock which led to the River Avon — it jammed!

It was only some adroit seamanship that enabled the ship to be pulled back without severe damage. One can imagine the heated scene that must have occurred in the ensuing emergency meeting between Brunel and the Dock Company directors. He must have told them in no uncertain terms what he was going to do, for the following night Brunel himself took charge of an army of workmen who removed coping stones and the lock gate platforms from the lock. With the benefit of a slightly higher tide, this allowed a tug to tow the ship safely into the River Avon, much to the great relief, no doubt, of everyone concerned.

As a result of these problems, which coincided with the halting of work on the Clifton Suspension Bridge, for a while Bristol became known as the city that built *"a bridge they couldn't finish and a ship they couldn't get out of the dock"*.

PRINCE STREET BRIDGE

The first Prince Street Bridge was built in 1809 by the Bristol Dock Company, prompted by the opening of the Floating Harbour, in that same year. It was a double-leaf wooden swing type with a slightly arched deck. A pair of toll houses in simple classical style flanked the gates. Masonry abutments (still there) were built out from each bank to reduce the span needed. It replaced the Gib (or Gibb) Ferry, owned and operated from mediaeval times by the monks of nearby St Augustine's Abbey – which became Bristol Cathedral. The ferry took its name from a man-powered dockside crane (gib is a variant of the word jib, the arm of a crane). The Bristol Dock Company collected the tolls from the bridge but was obliged to compensate the Abbey for loss of ferry revenue by passing on to them the tolls from pedestrians and handcarts. The Dock Company kept the tolls from livestock and wheeled traffic. On the opening of the bridge, the Bristol Mirror observed that *"by this road [Princes Street bridge to Cumberland Basin] the circuitous and disagreeable route to those fashionable watering places Hotwells and Clifton may be avoided and a safe, pleasant and picturesque one substituted in its stead"*.

After 70 years of service, the bridge was in poor condition. A report commissioned by the city corporation in 1876 found that the timbers were *"almost throughout so much worn and perished that if once taken apart for repair it will practically amount to entire renewal"*. The harbour railway company was concerned that the weight limits on the bridge were slowing down the speed of movement of goods. Apart from Clifton Suspension Bridge, it was the last existing toll bridge in the city. Bridge tolls had long been much resented by the citizens — indeed the original toll houses of this bridge were burned down in the Bristol Riot of 1831. The corporation resolved to buy out the ownership of the tolls, now owned by the Great Western Railway company, for £15,000, and to build a new toll-free bridge. The Docks Engineer, Mr Howard, ordered the water-hydraulic powered swing bridge we see today. It was built by Sir William Armstrong and Co. at a cost £3,400. A 75cm diameter hydraulic ram lifted the bridge about 7cm, using water at around 41 bars pressure, allowing it to swing open. The pumping engine (an "Otto" gas engine) and hydraulic accumulator were housed in two adjacent small buildings on the north bank which are still there and make an attractive pair. The pumping-engine house is made of rough-finished Pennant sandstone with limestone dressings and capped with a slate roof. The tall hydraulic accumulator tower is of cream-coloured timber weatherboarding. The bridge opened in January 1879. In front of several hundred people Mr George Wills, chair of the Docks Committee, pronounced it "...*one of the finest specimens of mechanical skill ever seen in Bristol*". The whole grouping is Grade II listed.

Two months after opening, the new bridge was the location of the very first large-scale public demonstration in Bristol of a new technology — electric light. The show was put on by The Pyramid Electric Lighting Company, under the supervision of, most appropriately, a Mr Brain, assisted by the city council's Mr Dayman. Four large carbon electrode arc-lamps were powered by four "Gramme" dynamos. Two of the dynamos were powered by the gas engine that pumped the bridge's hydraulics. A 6m high timber staging was erected just west of the bridge on the north bank, from which a lantern projected light up and down the harbour. On the south side of the bridge, another light illuminated Bathurst wharf, and two more lit up the inside of a transit shed. There was also a demonstration of how a person "*could convey force in the shape of a current through a wire*" by connecting a chaff-cutting machine on the south bank to a dynamo on the north bank via an insulated cable laid across the river bed. Sadly, the efforts of Mr Brain went down the drain — the Docks Committee stuck to gas. In the not-so-sagacious words of the Western Daily Press reporter "...*the craze for electric lighting was wearing off...*".

The bridge was closed for two years (2015–17) for extensive refurbishment costing well over £1m. Glass reinforced plastic (GRP) decking has replaced the original deck timbers. Twenty-four new bespoke steel beams, each a different size, were made and substituted for the originals. All three of the longitudinal girders were repaired. 1,000 cast iron ingots were removed from the counterbalance, cleaned and put back in the right place for the new balance and all the electrical and mechanical operating mechanisms were refurbished.

PERO'S BRIDGE

PERO'S BRIDGE

St Augustine's Reach is a man-made channel in the Floating Harbour. Created in the 13th century, it diverted the course of the River Frome from further upstream, near Bristol Bridge, in order to expand and improve the port facilities. It was a huge work of civil engineering that took eight years to complete and was probably the crucial factor that led to Bristol becoming England's second most important port (see p136).

The modern-day focal point of the Reach is an eye-catching asymmetrical single-leaf bascule bridge designed in 1993-4 by acclaimed Irish artist Eilis O'Connell, in collaboration with civil engineers Ove Arup & Partners and Bristol architects Childs and Sulzmann. A bascule bridge has counterweights that move downwards as the deck moves upwards. The distinctive horn-like counterweights of Pero's Bridge were built by the Bristol firm of Abels Shipbuilders Ltd. It was opened in 1999 by Home Office minister Paul Boateng. It was privately financed as a condition of planning consent for development of the Watersheds on the west bank of St Augustine's Reach.

Pero's Bridge is intended to be a work of art as well as a practical piece of infrastructure, forming part of a cycling/pedestrian route from Queen Square to Millenium Square. The sculptural asymmetric piers, clad in stainless steel, which support the deck are an integral part of the design, which was endorsed by the Royal Fine Art Commission. The outer spans at each end of the bridge are fixed, and were designed to be free from the clutter of supporting structure. The pattern in the surface of the cast-iron decking, sadly largely obscured by a later slapped-on non-slip coating, is similar to those in duct and grating covers which can be found in the pavements around the docks. The "horns" at each side of the bridge are the counterweights to the central leaf which is lifted by hydraulics. The curved ladder-like steelwork at the base of the horns are the surfaces on which they pivot with a rocking movement. As the horns move downwards and the central leaf rises, counterweight and deck also rock back a few feet, so that the deck does not have to be vertical to give the required clearances for river traffic. The length of the lifting span is 11m, which gives a nine metre wide navigation channel when open.

From a distance the bridge's silhouette is striking — the horns appropriately bring to mind nautical forms such as funnels, foghorns, speaking tubes or maybe some strange underwater plant or sea creature. Unfortunately, up close the horns have rough, uneven surfaces which make them look unfinished. This was certainly not intended by the artist but was not within her power to modify after fabrication.

In 2015, as part of the events celebrating Bristol's status as European Green Capital in that year, Japanese artist Fujiko Nakaya enveloped Pero's Bridge in a cloud of fog for a week by pumping water at high pressure through nozzles temporarily arranged around it. Her "fog works" have been seen in public spaces around the world, including Tokyo, San Francisco and New York City. "Fog Bridge" was intended to stimulate thoughts about climate change and our interaction with the environment.

The bridge is named in commemoration of Pero Jones, an enslaved African who was brought to live in Bristol, and is a reminder of the involvement of Bristol merchants in the slave trade. In the 1730s, Bristol was Britain's leading slave port. Pero Jones and his sisters, Nancy and Sheeba, were purchased as children by merchant John Pinney in 1765 for his Mountravers Plantation on the island of Nevis in the West Indies. Pero was 12–years–old. Pinney paid £115 (about £5,750 in today's money) for the three children and one adult slave. In 1784, Pinney brought Pero and the freed slave Frances Coker to Bristol where they lived in Great George Street. The house still exists ("The Georgian House") as a museum. Pero became Pinney's manservant and Frances became maid to Jane Pinney. Both servants visited Nevis in 1790 and Pero again in 1794. After this latter visit, according to Pinney, Pero started to drink heavily and his behaviour became unacceptable for one whose station in life was that of a servant. Pero fell ill in 1798, and to help him recuperate Pinney lodged him at Ashton, at that time surrounded by countryside. Pinney and his family visited him often. Pero was about 45 when he died and had served the Pinneys for 32 years. As far as is known, he was never given his freedom — he lived and died a slave.

REDCLIFFE BRIDGE

Redcliffe Bridge and Temple Bridge (chapter 4), were the first bridges in Bristol to be built solely to relieve traffic congestion.

In the mid-1930s, the city council decided to build a new eastern and a new western route around the central area. Temple and Redcliffe bridges were part of the plan. This route, built just as planned, entailed one of the greatest traffic planning crimes ever perpetrated in the UK — the driving of a dual-carriageway diagonally through Queen Square, which up to then was one of the best preserved Georgian squares in the country. Several old buildings in the opposite corners of the square had to be demolished. The route started at St

Augustine's Parade, joined up with Broad Quay, and after bashing through Queen Square, it crossed the river over the new bridge and joined up with the "Eastern Road" at the bottom of Redcliffe Street. It seems extraordinary now that, although there were 18 objections to the planning application for these proposals, they were all about compensation. Not a single one was about historical preservation! In 1939, regretfully, it all came to pass.

But just for once there has been a happy ending. Sixty-one years later, in 2000, tranquillity returned to Queen Square. The dual-carriageway was removed and the square was restored to a high standard — an achievement by the city that was widely recognised and acclaimed.

Redcliffe Bridge, as it came to be called, was completed in 1942. The main contractor was A E Parr, steelwork by Dorman Long and Head Wrightson and Co, and machinery by Thomas Bradshw & Sons. The whole of the technical design work for the bridge was done by the City Engineer H M Webb. The 4,000 tonne weight of the bridge is carried by 150 piles driven 6m below the riverbed. It is of the single-leaf Bascule (counterweighted) type — the rising part weighs 450 tonnes. In view of its sensitive position, close to St Mary Redcliffe, Sir George Oatley (architect of the Wills Tower) was called in as a consultant and the Royal Fine Arts Commission approved the final design. They thought it would be an "*acquisition to the city*". Hmmm. It's a rather severe affair that puts me in mind of civil defence. This is not surprising as only 12 months earlier, in World War Two, Bristol had taken a pounding from German bombers in which this bridge had a near-miss. A pier on the Welshback side still has the scars. St Philip's Bridge (chapter 2) took a direct hit. The two D-shaped control cabins that flank it in the middle resemble gun batteries or lookout posts. It seems to prefigure, by 20 years, the architectural style that would be called "Brutalism", which was partly influenced by the concrete constructions of World War Two. Redcliffe Bridge is now only opened very occasionally. It was refurbished in 1993.

There are good views from Redcliffe Bridge to the north along Welsh Back (left bank) and Redcliff Backs (right bank), towards Bristol Bridge. The "Backs" refer to the backs of merchants' houses from where goods were loaded directly to ships. Welsh Back was where ships from Wales were loaded. Looking south, Redcliffe Wharf is immediately on the left, followed by Phoenix Wharf. For decades, Redcliffe Wharf was the base for the Lucas Brothers, who traded with West Africa for palm oil, used in the manufacture of soap. Redcliffe takes its name from the red sandstone cliffs immediately behind Redcliffe Wharf and Phoenix Wharf. These cliffs are a rabbit warren of tunnels resulting from excavation of sand for the local glass–making industry and for ship's ballast. They were also used as store houses. Contary to urban myth, they were never used to house French Prisoners in the Napoleonic Wars.

126 | CASTLE BRIDGE

CASTLE BRIDGE

Castle Bridge, opened in April 2017, and thus one of Bristol's newest bridges, is located just a few hundred metres upstream of the oldest — Bristol Bridge — where the city of Bristol had its origins in Saxon times.

Provision of the bridge was a condition of planning consent obtained by the developer for Finzels Reach, a 2.4 ha site which encompasses most of the waterfront buildings opposite Castle Green, where Bristol Castle once stood. This development has turned buildings that were once part of Finzel's Sugar Refinery and the Courage Brewery into offices, housing, a hotel and leisure space. The bridge increases connectivity for pedestrians and cyclists from the city centre to both the new development and to Temple Meads railway station. The bridge's name was selected by a public vote from a shortlist of suggestions sent in by the general public.

The curved red brick facade that faces the bridge is the last remnant of the sugar refinery. In 1810, 17-year-old Conrad Finzel (1793–1859) had fled conscription into Napoleon's army and arrived in England as a penniless German migrant. He set about making his fortune. In 1839, he acquired the Counterslip Sugar House, founded in 1681 in the northeast part of the site, and expanded westwards along the waterfront. After a disastrous fire in 1846, he completely rebuilt the factory at huge cost, pledging to give a third of the profits to charity (he helped to support the orphanages run by his compatriot George Muller). At its peak, Finzel's Sugar Refinery was one of the largest in England and employed over 700 workers. After Finzel's death in 1859, his family kept Finzel & Sons going until 1877. A group of local businessmen then took over the refinery, but it finally closed, succumbing to competition from London, in 1881.

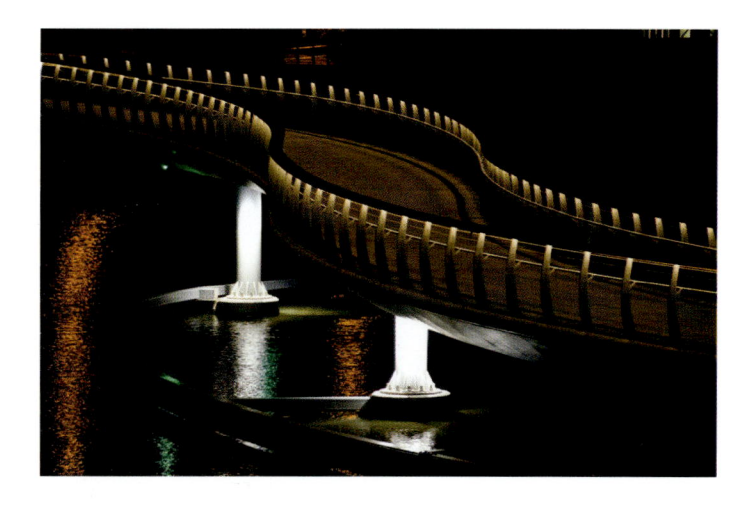

The motley collection of buildings east of the bridge (downstream) are the shells of some of the buildings of the former George's/Courage Brewery. Porter Brewery, on Bath Street, just behind the waterfront, was acquired in 1788 by a consortium which became the Philip George Bristol Porter and Beer Company. In 1796, the company built an adjacent new brewery. In 1861, the company became Georges and Company and by the early 20th century it was employing around 170 workers on this site. By 1933, the brewery covered 1.2 ha with an extensive waterfront facade and was then the largest brewery in the southwest. The company absorbed competitors to become the main brewer in Bristol. In 1961, it was taken over by Courage and then passed through various owners until it closed and became derelict in 1991.

Castle Bridge was designed by Bristol architects The Bush Consultancy, with international firm WSP and CTS Bridges of Huddersfield as consulting engineers. Fabrication was also by CTS Bridges and installation was by Andrew Scott Ltd, of North Yorkshire. The cost was £2.5m. It is 91m long and 4m wide. It was a complex challenge for both designers and builders.

The primary factor governing the overall form of the bridge was the 7m difference in ground levels between the two banks. A bridge that went horizontally across the river from Castle Green would require steps and a lift on the other side. To avoid this inconvenience to users, it was decided that the bridge would have a smooth gradient from one riverbank to the other. Since the maximum desired slope was 1 in 20, this required a long total span that could not be the shortest distance across the water. The result is the delightful meandering path that provides the user with the unusual experience of walking, not across the river, but *along* it. The deck and parapet steelwork is cantilevered from a central spine comprising a pair of braced universal beams which create a torsion box. It curves simultaneously in all three dimensions necessitating the use of some fancy 3D design software. The curves of the fibreglass panels that clad the underside of the deck were designed with a program used for sportscar bodywork.

There were 1,000 individual parts to the bridge which were prefabricated into four sections, weighing up to 25 tonnes each, delivered by road to a holding area near Temple Meads station. From here, they were put on pontoons on the river and brought to the site where they were hoisted into place by a floating crane. Every time the crane was moved, it took an hour for the stabilising legs to settle through 7m of silt to find a purchase on the riverbed. Divers assisted in underwater inspections. The harbour walls are historic artifacts which must be kept free of loads and so the weight of the bridge is almost wholly supported on 13 750mm–diameter reinforced concrete piles which penetrate 6m into the mudstone bedrock beneath 7m of silt! The piles were screwed rather than hammered in so as not to disturb local peregrine falcons during the construction work. The lighting of the bridge is designed so as not to disturb bats that use the course of the river as a flightpath. The ferry landing stage on the north bank was redesigned, and new planting was carried out.

From a number of angles Castle Bridge looks rather squeezed in to a tight space, but the need for a combined pedestrian and cycle route determined its 4m minimum width. The protective barriers at water level add to the clutter, but again, they are unfortunately obligatory. Despite these quibbles, Castle Bridge is an elegant and worthy addition to the waterscape of the Floating Harbour. Its gentle and subtle curves sit low across the water and it does not impose itself unduly on a very "sensitive" and historic area. It has deservedly won awards from Bristol Civic Society and the Institute of Civil Engineers.

THE KÖNIGSBERG BRIDGE PROBLEM
Thilo Gross

In 2011, I moved to Bristol to teach Engineering Mathematics at Bristol University. An important topic in the curriculum is the mathematics of complex networks, a branch of maths that is essential for understanding the many complex systems that surround us. The story of "network maths" starts with a single problem that is mentioned in every textbook on the subject: the Königsberg Bridge Problem.

You will not find Königsberg in a modern atlas, as the former Prussian city is now known by its Russian name: Kaliningrad. It lies on the river Pregel, where it occupies land around two river islets. In the 18th century, the islets and the banks of the river were connected by seven beautiful bridges, all quite close together (Fig 1). A pleasant way of spending a fine Sunday morning was to go for a stroll across all the seven bridges. And, wouldn't it be preferable not to have to cross over a bridge you have already crossed?

Königsberg is a university town and home to famous intellectuals such as Immanuel Kant, and later, David Hilbert. But, surprisingly, nobody seemed to be able to find a route that carried the walker over all the bridges which did not involve crossing one of them multiple times. The bridge problem became a famous puzzle that was widely known throughout Europe: is it possible to find a route that crosses every bridge just once?

In 1736, the mayor of Danzig asked the Swiss mathematician Leonhard Euler (1707–1783) if he would try to solve the problem. Euler (pronounced "Oiler") was the preeminent mathematician of his time and is still counted among the greatest mathematicians in history. He contributed so many concepts to mathematics that Wikipedia has a dedicated page for "Things named after Euler". Among them is the "Eulerian Walk", the walk that crosses every bridge only once.

To Euler's contemporaries, and perhaps even many modern readers, finding a route across a set of bridges may not seem like a mathematical problem at all. For starters, it does not seem to contain any numbers; but maths is not a science of numbers, it is a way of structured thinking that can be applied to a vast variety of problems.

In Euler's time, the only type of mathematics without numbers was geometry, but Euler realised that classical geometry would not solve the bridge problem. It was too concerned with where things were exactly, whereas the bridge problem was about where things were relative to each other — how they were connected. He invented a new way of mathematical thinking that he called the "geometry of position".

Using the geometry of position, Euler found a solution to the bridge problem

Leonard Euler by Jakob Emanuel Handmann (1753). © Rudolf Bischoff-Merian

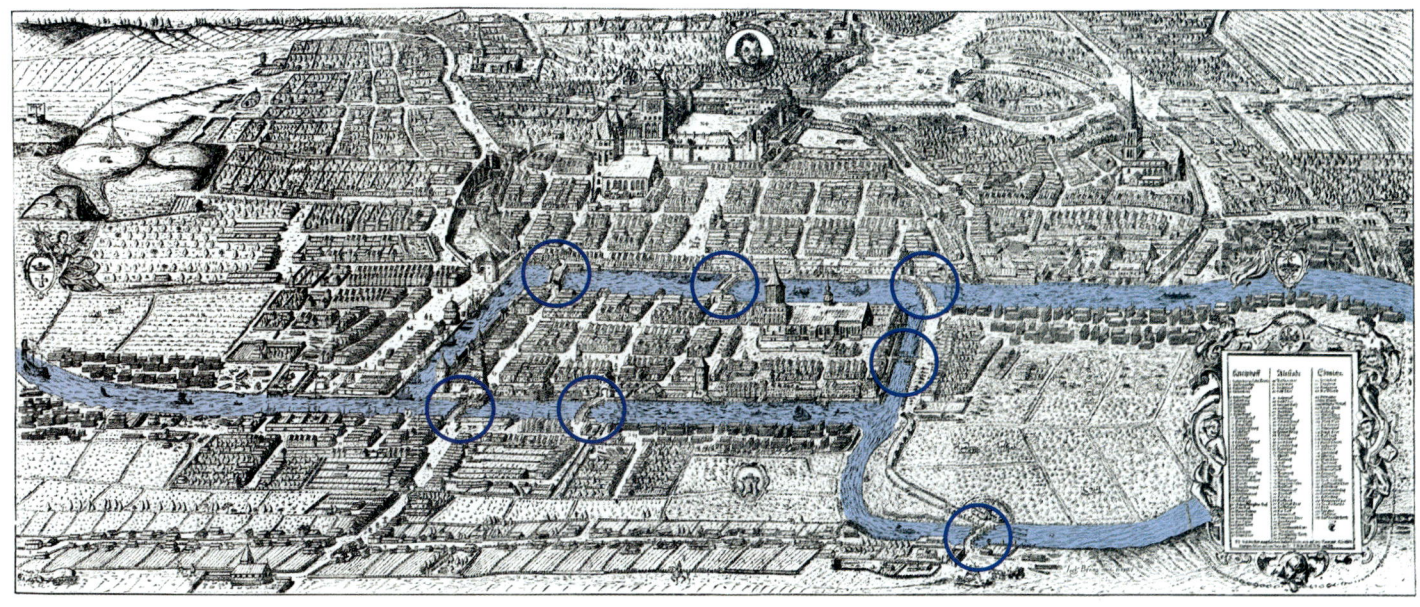

Fig. 1. The seven bridges of 18th century Königsberg taken from Köenigsberg map by Bering, 1613.

(explained below) that was felt to be so beautiful that it inspired similar analysis and kick-started whole new branches of mathematics: topology — the maths of the structure of things; graph theory — the mathematical study of networks; and the overarching framework of "discrete mathematics", the mathematics of undividable objects. Thus the bridge problem, a simple mathematical puzzle, played a central role in laying the foundation for a large number of fields of modern mathematics. Among these is network science, an interdisciplinary field that powers modern companies, such as Google and Facebook, and informs decisions in a vast spectrum of applications, ranging from biology and medicine to the operation of large technical systems.

Euler's solution to the Königsberg Bridge Problem

The key to the bridge problem is to realise that much of the information that is captured by a normal map is not important for the problem. We do not need to care about the precise topography of the river, the layout of the streets of Königsberg or the location of particular buildings. What matters are the different land masses and how they are connected by bridges.

Searching for a suitable walk becomes much easier if we make a simpler map that does not include needless information that could otherwise distract us (Fig. 2). But even this highly simplified map of Königsberg contains more than the bare minimum of information. Can we go further?

We do not actually need to know the size or shape of the different land masses, so we can represent them by blobs of identical size, which we will call "nodes". So, there are four nodes (let's call them a, b, c, d, see Fig. 2) representing the north and south side of the river and the two islands. In addition to the land masses, we need to indicate the bridges. We do this by representing each bridge with a line between the nodes connected by the bridge. We call these lines links. With

Fig. 2. A cleaned–up map of Königsberg.

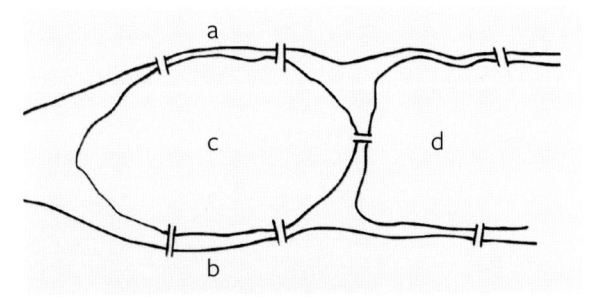

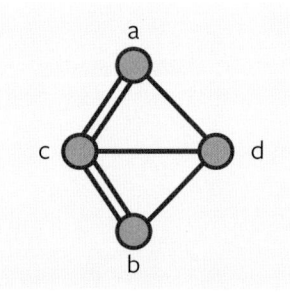

Fig. 3. Network representation of Königsberg.

Fig. 4. Nodes of degree 1, 2, 3, and 4.

these final simplications, our map of Königsberg has become a set of nodes and links, i.e. a network (Fig. 3).

Now that we have a better map, we can start thinking about the actual problem. Using the diagram in Fig. 3, you can try to find a solution by trial and error — but you won't find one. Most attempts will come very close to a solution; you will have crossed all but one bridge when you trap yourself on an island that you cannot leave without crossing a bridge twice.

After some failed attempts, one starts to wonder, is there a solution at all? And, if there isn't one, can we at least prove that no solution exists? The appearance of the word "prove" makes this a mathematical problem, and to solve this problem we need to stop thinking how we could find a walk, and start thinking about how we fail.

In the bridge problem, the only way to fail is to trap yourself in a node (i.e. an island or a river bank) that you can't leave without using a bridge a second time. This would happen, for example, if there was a node which had one link connecting to it. To reach such a place, we would cross its only bridge and then we couldn't leave again. A node with two bridges poses no such problem — we can arrive via one bridge and leave via the other.

If a node connects to three links, we will have to visit it twice. On our first visit we use one bridge to arrive and one bridge to leave. On the second visit we use the third and last bridge to arrive, and we are trapped! A node connecting to four bridges poses no such problem — we can arrive twice and leave twice using all four bridges only once.

This pattern continues: all nodes on which the number of endpoints of bridges is even pose no problem. But the nodes on which the number of endpoints of bridges is odd must be either the start or the end of our walk. In mathematical language, the number of endpoints of links on a node is said to be the *degree* of the node.

Based on the reasoning above we can say: *If a node has odd degree, an Eulerian walk (if one exists) starts in the node or ends there.*

This means if a walk that crosses every bridge only once is possible, any node with odd degree must either be the start or the end of that walk.

Because every walk only has one start and one end point, this means that an Eulerian walk is not possible if there are more than two nodes of odd degree. By contrast, one can show that, if the number of nodes of odd degree is two or less, we cannot fail if we choose our path wisely.

We have discovered a simple rule that allows us to decide if a Eulerian Walk is possible in a given network. So, let's consider Königsberg again. By counting the number of endpoints of links, we find that all four nodes have an odd degree (Fig. 3) and this proves that an Eulerian walk is not possible. Bad news for historical Königsberg, but what about Bristol?

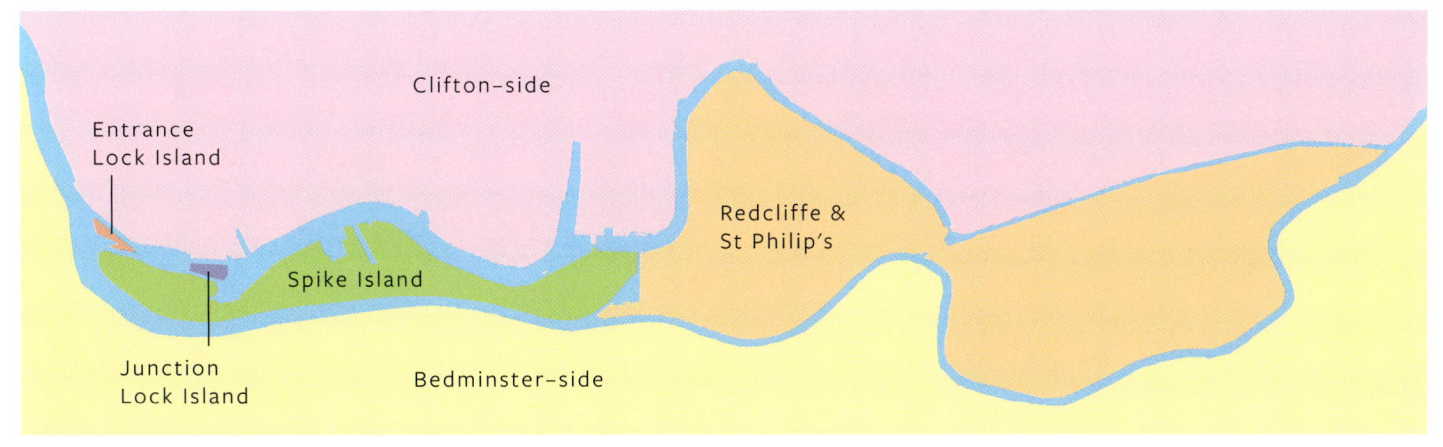

Fig. 5: Bristol, like Königsberg, occupies the land around a river with two major islands, but has two extra little ones, making a total of six nodes (four islands and two riverbanks).

The Bristol Bridge Problem

When I arrived in Bristol, I was struck by its similarity to Königsberg. The two cities are similar in size and are a similar distance from the coast. Historical parallels exist. And Bristol, like Königsberg, has two major islands (sort of) in its river (Fig. 5).

During one of my first lectures in Bristol, I mentioned this similarity. My Engineering Mathematics students immediately demanded to know if an Eulerian walk was possible: could one go on a single continuous walk that crossed every bridge in the city without crossing any bridge twice? Solving this question turned out to be far more work that I had expected.

The first challenge was to find the bridges. I spent hours trying to identify bridges in maps and satellite images, and then went on several exploratory walks to check whether I could cross them. Nevertheless, my first attempt to do the Eulerian walk failed because I discovered another bridge while walking and ended up trapping myself on St Philips.

I also encountered another problem. What actually counts as a bridge? Some bridges cannot be legally crossed on foot because they only carry train tracks or motorways. Some crossings are not really bridges, because the river or stream that is being crossed disappears into a pipe and resurfaces only some distance away. Some bridges cross roads or railways and not water, and some of the bridges, like Bedminster Bridge, could be counted as either one or two bridges. On closer examination, what we call a bridge started to seem quite arbitrary. So, which ones should I include in the puzzle?

I had almost given up on the problem when I had a sudden insight: one should be asking which bridges would have been included in the orginal Königsberg problem? This immediately led me to the following rules:

1. The bridges included should be within the city boundary.
2. They should be legally walkable by the general public.
3. They should cross a major waterway, i.e. the River Avon, the New Cut, the Floating Harbour or the Feeder Canal.
4. Separate structures count as separate bridges (this means that there are two Bedminster bridges).

Note that the third rule implies that small bridges that cross tributaries are excluded. Such smaller bridges also existed around Königsberg and were not included in the

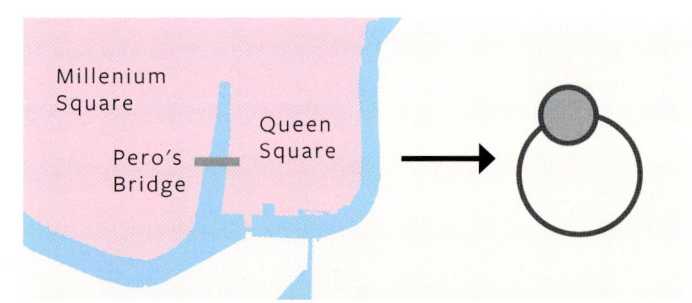

Fig. 6: Both ends of Pero's Bridge are on the Clifton side of the Floating Harbour. It forms a "loop" in the network.

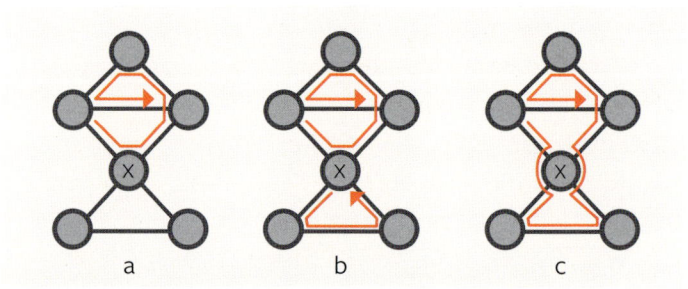

Fig. 7: An Eulerian walk can be found by Hierholzer's algorithms.

original puzzle. However, in Bristol some of the bridges that cross tributaries are historically significant and I have included these for good measure. If you think these count as part of the puzzle, it is good that I have included them. If you think they should not count, it does not matter how often we cross them so we can cross them anyway! None of these extra bridges are essential for the solution as one can always walk around the tributary with relative ease, but some are fantastic bridges, so let's walk them.

After many hours of online research, and more exploratory trips, I was satisfied that I had found all the bridges. One peculiarity of Bristol is that some bridges connect a land mass to itself and form "loops" in the network. For example, Pero's Bridge, close to the Watershed, connects to the north bank (the Clifton side of the river) at both its ends (Fig. 6).

Fortunately, the existence of such loops does not complicate the puzzle. Because we compute the degree of a node by counting the endpoints, a loop at a node increases the degree by two. This means it never turns an odd node into an even node or vice versa.

At the time of my first Bristol bridge walk, the Clifton side of the river and Spike Island had an odd degree, while the Bedminster side and Redcliffe had an even degree. The small Entrance Lock and Junction Lock islands had, and still have, a degree of two. In summary, there were only two nodes of odd degree: an Eulerian walk was possible, I only had to find it.

Finding walks

If a walk is possible, we can find it using a method known as "Hierholzer's Algorithm". In a nutshell, the idea of this method is to try to find a walk, fail, and learn from the failure. Let me illustrate it with a small example network (Fig. 7).

If there are nodes of odd degree, we must start in one of them. We then try to do the walk. If we are lucky or clever enough, we may find the walk straight away. But suppose we failed. In this case, your walk must have passed through at least one node that has some unused bridges left. Let's give this node a name, X (Fig. 7 [a]). We can now try the following: go on a second walk that starts at X and crosses as many bridges as possible, without using any bridge that we used in the first attempt. By some mathematical magic, the only place where we can trap ourselves on the second walk is X (Fig. 7 [b]). So, the second walk will always be a circular walk.

We have now made two attempts, each of which has crossed different bridges. Learning from those attempts allows us to go on a walk that crosses each bridge that was crossed in either of the previous two attempts. Here is how: start at the original starting point of the first attempt and follow the route of the first attempt until you reach X. From X, follow the route of the second attempt; because the second attempt was a circular walk, it will bring us back to X. Now that we have returned to X, we can follow the rest of the route of the first attempt (Fig. 7 [c]).

We have now found a route that crosses each bridge that was crossed in any of the first two attempts just once. In many cases, this will be the solution. If it is not the solution yet, we can repeat the same trick. There must be an island that is visited by the third attempt that has unused bridges left; we call this Y, and go for another walk starting from Y that does not use any bridge that was used in the first or second attempts. This walk will be circular. So we can merge it with the previous route, using the same trick as above, to find a route that crosses yet more bridges. Even in very stubborn networks, repeating this procedure a couple of times will find a solution that crosses every bridge only once (assuming such a solution exists).

Hierholzer's Algorithm gives you a solution. But for every given set of bridges, there will generally be many different walks that cross every bridge only once. When it is your own feet that do the walking, you want to find a solution that is also going to fit certain criteria such as minimising both the distance walked and the chances of being hit by a car, taking in as many of the sights of the city as possible and avoiding the boring bits. Surprisingly, I found there isn't an extensive mathematical literature on "optimising" the route of the bridge walk. So I had to develop a procedure for myself, and eventually came up with my own algorithm which led to the route described in this book.

Working out just how many Euler walks exist for a given set of islands and bridges, or any other kind of network, remains an unsolved mathematical problem that, if solved, could have important implications for a much wider range of applications. If you are up to the challenge, give it a try. You might make mathematical history!

Walking the Bristol bridgewalk

On Feb 23rd, 2013, I went on an 11-hour, 33-mile Eulerian walk through Bristol that took me over each of the bridges only once.

Originally I had planned the walk only for my own enjoyment, but I told some friends and students about it. The university wrote a press release and before I knew it, the story of the bridge walk received double-page coverage in the Bristol Post. Other media coverage followed, including a radio interview, but in particular an article by Jeff Lucas in the Bristol Civic Society's "Better Bristol" magazine sparked a lot of interest. I started receiving frequent requests for the exact route. People used it for several charity events or walked it for fun with friends.

Since 2013, many things have changed in Bristol, and a number of new bridges have been built. In response, the bridge walk has changed several times and, for a short while, actually became impossible. At the time of writing, we have reached a time of relative stability. More importantly, the walk is better than ever. Due to recently built bridges, all nodes now have even degree, so a circular walk has become possible, and it is even slightly shorter than the original walk.

BRISTOL'S WATERWAYS — A VERY BRIEF HISTORY

It is hard to imagine the city centre as a bustling port crammed with shipping, but that is what it once was for over a thousand years, and for much of that time second only to the port of London in importance. Since the birth of the city of Bristol in Saxon times, its waterways have been subjected to two major events of re-engineering, both of which substantially increased the capacity of the port and had considerable influence on its subsequent appearance and history.

The first major change came in the 13th century. Up untill then, ships had berthed just downstream of Bristol Bridge, where the River Frome used to join the Avon. Baldwin Street roughly follows its old course. A bigger and better harbour was created by diverting the course of the River Frome so that its confluence with the Avon was at the south end of a 0.7km long trench, 5.5m deep, 35m wide, dug entirely by hand. The remaining visible part is what we know as St Augustine's Reach. This created Broad Quay and Narrow Quay. At that time, it was an extraordinary feat of engineering that took eight years to complete. It was equivalent to building a major castle or cathedral and it probably was crucial in making Bristol the second most important port in England for hundreds of years. Most of it is now covered over, but the Frome still flows in an underground culvert from the centre to an outlet into the Avon, near Gaol Ferry bridge. The Reach takes its name from the then landowner, St Augustine's Abbey (now Bristol Cathedral).

The second big change came 600 years later, in 1804–9. For a thousand years, the major problem with the Port of Bristol had been the inconvenient fact that, twice a day, most of the water in the port disappeared when the tide went out — the tidal range at Bristol is about 9m. Ships would tip over (awkward), the timbers would dry out (weakening them), and loading/unloading could not be carried out (wasting time). Eventually, in 1803, a renowned civil engineer, William Jessop, was engaged to put a stop to the problem by implementing his hugely ambitious and expensive plan to remedy it.

His plan comprised the following:

1. The existing course of the River Avon through the city, from Rownham to the western end of St Philip's Marsh, would be turned into a tide-free artificial lake of 30ha. by damming it at Rownham. This was termed the "Floating Harbour", as ships would now float in it permanently.
2. A new channel, the "New Cut", 3.5km long, would be dug for the River Avon, south of the original course, to bypass the dammed section.
3. A new canal 1.6km long, "The Feeder", would bring relatively silt-free fresh water from the Avon at Netham (usually below the reach of the silty tide) into the Floating Harbour at Totterdown. A weir would regulate the water level in the harbour. The canal would be a route into the city for barges.
4. Entrance locks for major shipping coming up the Avon would be sited at the Rownham end of the Floating Harbour.
5. A large semi-tidal basin, "Cumberland Basin", would be created immediately behind the main entrance locks, as

a holding area for ships waiting to leave the harbour. A "Juction Lock" between it and the rest of the harbour would enable the basin to be used as a lock.

6. A new basin for smaller craft, "Bathurst Basin", would be created at Treen Mills where the River Malago entered the Avon. Entrance locks into the basin would be sited at each end of it.
7. A further secondary set of locks, for smaller craft, would be sited where the New Cut ran close to the Floating Harbour at Totterdown — called "Calcraft" or "Totterdown Lock" (it no longer exists).
8. An "overfall dam" just east of the Junction Lock would allow the water level in the harbour to be controlled at its west end, and permit a continous flow of water through the harbour to keep it clean and silt-free (in theory).

The creation of the New Cut, in particular, was an enormous work of civil engineering, carried out by an army of itinerant workmen — the "navvies". Although explosives were now in use to blast out the channel, and steam power was used to lift stone out of the cut, a huge amount of digging and all the clearing of the rubble had to be done by pick and shovel. No pneumatic drills. No JCB's.

The construction work for Jessop's Scheme started in 1804 and was largely completed by 1809. The total cost was £600,000, equivalent to around £50m today. This is pretty good value, but we must bear in mind that a significant cost of the project was labour which, at that time, came very cheap.

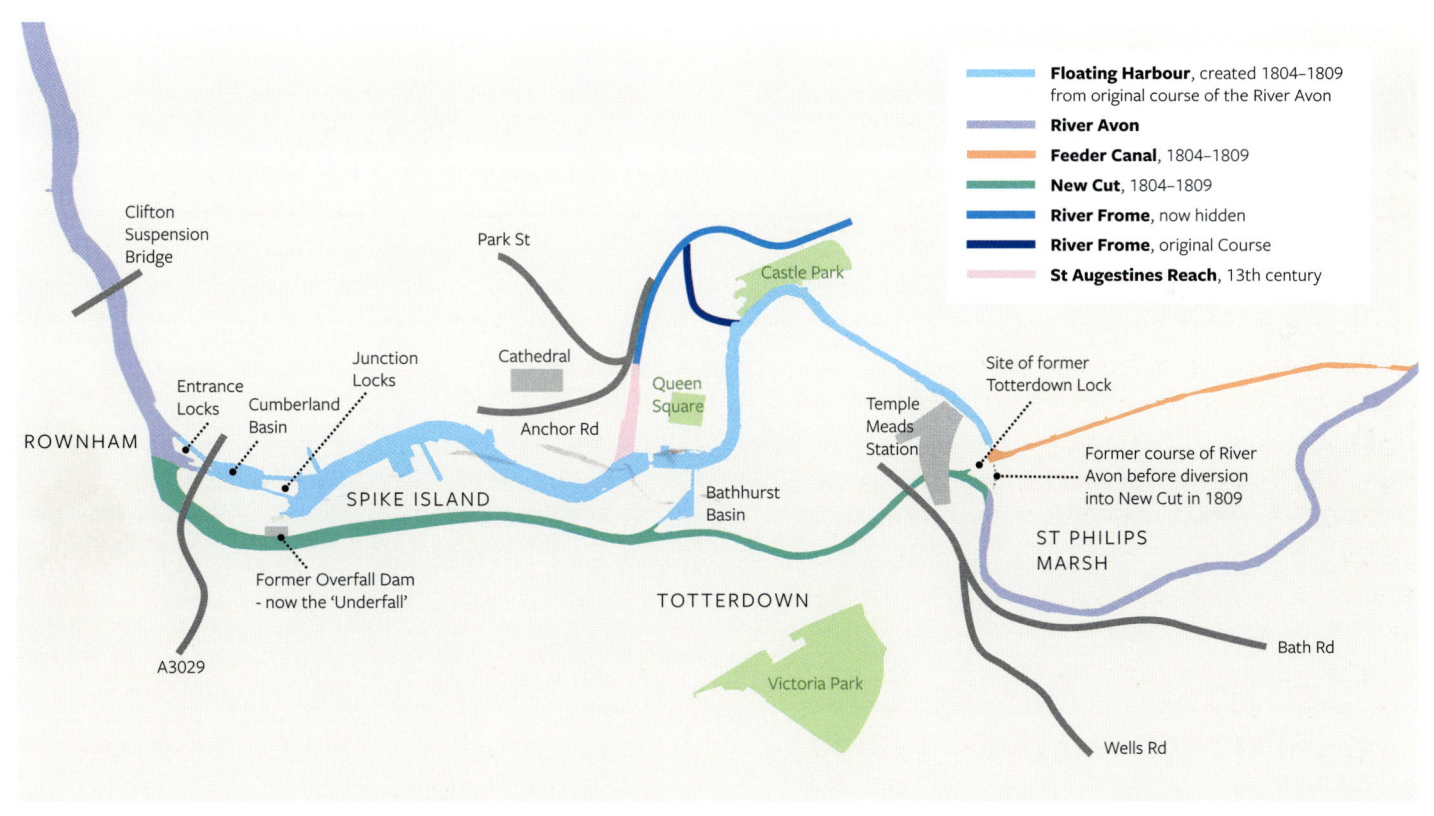

BRISTOL'S WATERWAYS – A VERY BRIEF HISTORY | 137

WALK INSTRUCTIONS

These instructions are to guide you from bridge to bridge, and they begin where it seems most appropriate to start the walk — at Bristol's first bridge. They are not intended to be a guided tour of the whole city, but some items of significant interest that you pass along the way are pointed out. The walk is circular, so you could choose your own preferred starting (and finishing) point if this would be more convenient. Many people will be tempted to omit the long Clifton–Avonmouth–Clifton "loop" along the course of the Avon, but this section of the walk is richly rewarding and takes you through some delightful and varied scenery. I urge you not to miss this out! The section from Avonmouth Bridge to Clifton takes you over some rough ground and parts of it it can be very muddy in wet weather. Sensible shoes are a must.

Much use is made in these instructions of compass directions, so it is a good idea to take a compass/GPS. And just to be clear, "Downstream" = same direction as flow of river, "Upstream" = opposite direction to flow of river.

The distances between bridges are given in the list on the map on page 8.

These instructions, the map and a .gpx file, can be downloaded free from the Bristol Books website and The Bristol Bridges Walk Challenge Facebook Page.

▶ www.bristolbooks.org/new-products/from-brycgstow-to-bristol-in-45-bridges

---

The walk begins at Castle Green. Before you start, take a look at the ruined St Peters Church. Note how (in the absence of other buildings) it gives an excellent all round view of the environs. It is likely that the Saxons made a settlement here and thus began Bristol. Now make your way down to the southwest corner of the park, to Bridge Street.

1. From Bridge Street cross **Bristol Bridge (1)** to Victoria Street

On your way across, upstream on your left you see one of Bristol's newest bridges, Castle Bridge. This will be the last bridge you cross if you do the whole walk. Until the Second World War Victoria Street was Bristol's main shopping street. Just ahead on the right is the enormous grey bulk of the Robinson Building (1963), Bristol's first high-rise office block, followed by a small row of gabled houses dating from 1675 (the date of 1485 on the wall refers to a previous building). You will pass some fine restored Victorian buildings on your left.

2. Walk along Victoria Street for 150m and turn left into Countership. Follow Countership and cross **St Philip's Bridge (2)** on the left pavement.

As you cross the bridge you see Temple Bridge upstream on your right, and behind it, Valentine's Bridge.

3. Immediately after St Philip's Bridge take the stairs to your left down to the waterside and walk towards Castle Park for 200m until you arrive at **Castle Ditch Bridge (3)**.

From here you now have a good view of Castle Bridge a little way downstream.

4. Cross Castle Ditch Bridge then turn right. Follow the path till you reach Queen Street, turn right and follow it to Passage Street. Turn left onto Passage Street (which becomes Narrow Plain) and follow it to Temple Way.

Just before Temple Way on the left is the church of Sts Philip and Jacob. Parts date from around 1200 but it was very altered in the 18th and 19th centuries.

5. Turn right onto Temple Way. Keep on the right side and follow it to **Temple Bridge (4)**.

St Philip's bridge is downstream, and Valentine's Bridge can be seen upstream.

6. Cross the bridge and at the end of the parapet wall take the ramp on your right, down to the water. Turn right and walk underneath the bridge. As you emerge, walk between the two red brick pillars and in about 200m you will arrive at **Valentine's Bridge (5)**.

7. Cross Valentine's Bridge, then immediately turn right and continue along Glass Wharf to **Meads Reach Bridge (6)**.

You will pass a pair of tall grey funnel shaped objects next to the water — this is an artwork called "The Freetank" by Roger Hiorns and refers to the glassmaking history of this area.

8. Cross Meads Reach Bridge and continue straight on towards the train sheds of Temple Meads station in front of you. In 200m when you reach the street called "Friary", turn left and walk up a ramp towards Temple Meads station.

You pass across the open end of a car park in Sir Matthew Digby Wyatt's extension (1871–8) to Brunel's original train shed (1839–41) which is on the other side of the timber partition wall at the far end.

9. Enter the station through the door with the sign 'Booking Offices' above, then immediately leave through the main doors on the right. Walk

down Station Approach to Temple Gate.

The glass canopies of the station front Wyatt's 1870's building in reddish stonework. Brunel's original station building, in light grey stonework, is on your right, after the opening with "Passenger Shed" above it. On the other side of the carpark is the handsome Jacobean-style former headquarters of the Bristol and Exeter Railway (1852-4) designed by S C Fripp.

10. Cross Temple Gate at the traffic lights, turn left and follow it to **Bath Bridges — East and West (7) (8)**. Cross western Bath Bridge (newer, uninteresting), then follow the loop of the roundabout back and cross eastern Bath Bridge (older, interesting).

From the bridge, looking east, you can see Temple Meads station and the major railway bridge that carries the platforms.

11. After crossing both sides of Bath Bridge, turn right onto Cattle Market Road and pass underneath the platforms of Temple Meads station. On the other side of the platforms (the Cattle Market would have been on the left here) cross the road and continue on the small path towards **Brock's Bridge(9)**.

A few metres along this path, as you approach Brock's Bridge, you pass a channel cut into the riverbank on your right, blocked with debris. This was Totterdown Lock, which was the entrance from the river into the far eastern end of the Floating Harbour. There was a bridge over the entrance channel called Feeder Road Bridge. The channel was blocked in World War II to prevent the Floating Harbour being drained of water in the event of a bomb hitting the lock gates.

12. At the time of going to press, both Brock's Bridge and St Philip's footbridge are not open to the public, pending further development on Temple Island. For the time being divert accordingly to reach Temple Meads Relief Line Bridge.

13. Cross Brock's Bridge, turn left. After 200m you arrive at **St Philip's Footbridge (10)**. Cross the bridge and turn right along the riverside path until you reach the **Temple Meads Relief Line Bridge (11)**. Take the stairs to your right and cross over the bridge.

14. Walk uphill to Bath Road. Turn left onto Bath Road (note the fine early 19th century signpost called the Three Lamps) and follow it towards Bath.

After about 200m, on the right you pass the Thunderbolt Pub with the spiky barge boards, a Grade 11 Listed Victorian pub formerly called the Turnpike, named after the Totterdown Turnpike gate (long demolished), located near where travellers entering the city along this road had to pay a fee. A few metres further on that side is Summer Street, which gives an interesting view up to Holy Nativity Church (1883, rebuilt 1958) with its distinctive green copper spire.

On the left you pass Totterdown Bridge which you cross later. 50m further on, opposite the bus stop, is a fine Victorian Italianate tenement building, and following that is a long handsome Victorian terrace row with attractive stone decoration on the triple height bay windows.

15. Leave Bath Road by veering left and enter The Paintworks, "Bristol's Creative Quarter". In 200m turn left at a big colourful 3D sign with PAINT in large white letters. At the river, turn right and walk upstream for 200m to **Sparke Evans Park Bridge (12)**.

16. Cross the bridge into Sparke Evans Park and descend the ramp.

A short detour in the park of 100m downstream (going west) will bring you to a copse, on the east side of which is a (very dilapidated) Edwardian bandstand, with some fine decorative cast iron columns and corbels.

17. At the bottom of the Sparke Evans Bridge ramp turn right and follow the path upstream (east) out of the park to the **St Philips Causeway Bridges (East and West) (13) (14)**. Take the upper path underneath both bridges then take the steps on the left up to street level.

18. Cross the east bridge on the upstream side first. Make your way clockwise around the roundabout by crossing three busy roads, and then cross the western downstream bridge. At the end of the bridge use the traffic lights to turn right and cross the two roads.

At some time in the future it may be possible to take a riverside footpath eastwards starting below the east bridge which will avoid having to walk through the Avon Meads Retail Park. Although there is a metal gate to tempt you at the start of this path it is currently (2019) a dead end.

19. Head into the retail park and follow the line of shops on your right. Pass to the left of the Showcase Cinema (railway now behind a fence on your left) and turn left under a railway bridge, then immediately right along Cole Road, with the dramatic elevated Spine Road ahead of you, until you get to Feeder Road. Turn right under another railway bridge and follow the Canal upstream to **Barton Hill Bridge (15)**. From here you can see Silverthorne Lane footbridge a little way downstream.

20. Cross Barton Hill Bridge and immediately turn right. Follow the footpath through Netham Park to **Netham Lock Bridge (East) (16)**.

21. At the lock, cross both roads and then turn right to cross the east bridge. Don't use the west bridge just yet, but, turn left and continue for 50m to **New Brislington Bridge (17)**.

From the bridge you have a good view of Netham Wier, downstream.

22. As soon as you are over the bridge take the gravel path on the left (past a stubby metal bollard) upstream along the river to **St Anne's Footbridge (18)**.

23. Cross St Anne's Footbridge and then turn left to follow the riverside path downstream back to Netham Lock.

On your left you will have a good view of the entrance to the Feeder Canal.

24. As you come to the Netham bridges again, cross the first road and then turn left to cross the **Netham Lock Bridge (West) (19)**. Turn immediately right on the right hand pavement of the Feeder Road which you now follow for some while.

In about 200m on the right you will pass a freight container in camoflage colours with a "green" roof. This houses the Feeder Canal Sand Martin Colony and is also a work of art. Carry on past Barton Hill Bridge, which we crossed earlier, underneath a railway bridge and the second St. Philips Causeway Bridge. As as you pass under the latter, you can enjoy it's crisp, chunky concrete support columns and the undulating lines of the deck support girders. Next come some pipe and conveyor bridges wrapped in beige corrugated sheeting. (None of these are walkable by the public and are excluded).

25. At **Feeder Road Footbridge (20)**, cross the Feeder Canal into Barton Hill. Follow the footpath to Silverthorne Lane, and turn left.
Immediately on your left is an impressive stone built Victorian Factory/Warehouse.

26. Follow Silverthorne Lane left around the corner, where it intersects with Gas Lane and Kingsland Road, but cross over to the pavement on the right side of Silverthorne Road.
On the corner are the very fine former offices of the John Lysaght Galvanising Works, faced in beige coloured smooth sandstone (1891-3). A few metres further on are wonderful Victorian Disneyesque main gates (Rundbogenstil, to be precise).

27. Carry on along Silverthorne Lane and at the T-junction turn left.
Straight in front of you at the T-junction is the huge stone-built former Avon Street Gas Works Retort House (1850s), now a nightclub.

28. Follow Avon Street to **Marsh bridge (21)**.

29. Cross Marsh Bridge and continue straight on Albert Road. Follow Albert Road around the bend then turn right at the next intersection towards **Totterdown Bridge (22)**.

30. Cross Totterdown Bridge, cross Bath Road and turn right. Follow Bath Road a short stretch to the Intersection with Angers Road.

31. Turn left into Angers Road and follow it all the way steeply uphill to its intersection with Wells Road. At Wells Road turn left, and in 50m cross at the pedestrian crossing in front of the old Lloyds Bank.

32. Turn right and use the crossing at the top of St John's Lane. Pass to the left of the island of shops into the upper part of Oxford Street. At the Oxford pub on the left, turn left onto Cheapside Street.

33. At the end of Cheapside Street turn right and immediately left onto Windsor Terrace.
Victoria Park is straight ahead in the distance.

34. At the end of Windsor Terrace turn right onto St Lukes Road and follow it along the edge of Victoria Park, under a railway bridge and carry straight on to **Langton Street (Banana) Bridge (23)**.

35. Cross Langton Street Bridge and then turn left to follow the river to **Bedminster Bridges (East and West) (24) (25)**.

36. Turn left to cross eastern Bedminster Bridge (newer, uninteresting), then follow the roundabout around to western Bedminster Bridge (older, interesting) and cross the river again.
At the western bridge, if you turn round and face south, across Coronation Road behind some trees, is the handsome former Zion Congregational Chapel, (1830).

A few metres to the east of the bridge on the north bank is a Victorian drinking fountain, a listed structure, dated 1861, pre-dating this bridge by 20 years. It has a cast iron shell-shaped bowl and a marble splashback.

37. Cross Cumberland Road and carry straight on along the left side of Redcliffe Way. Turn left into Guinea Street and follow it to **Bathurst Basin Footbridge (26)**.

38. Cross Bathurst Basin Footbridge and turn left to walk along Bathurst Basin to **Bathurst Basin Roadbridges (East and West) (27) (28)**.

39. Use the pedestrian walkway on the side of east Bathurst Basin Roadbridge (older, interesting) to cross the entrance to Bathurst Basin, and then recross the water over west Bathurst Basin Roadbridge (newer, uninteresting).

40. Turn left onto Cumberland Road and follow it downstream.
At the start of Cumberland Road on the north side is a high stone wall. This is the remains of the outer wall of the city's "New Gaol", completed 1820, destroyed in the Bristol Reform Bill Riots of 1831, then rebuilt. A few metres down the road is the old gateway with an arch and two flanking towers. Public hangings took place on the walkway between the towers, sometimes in front of a crowd of thousands.

41. After a short stretch we reach **Gaol Ferry Bridge (29)**. Cross Gaol Ferry bridge.
Turn left and walk in the direction of St John's Church for about 40m and there is a gap in the railings where a track leads you down in a zig-zag 6 or 7m below the bridge. Stop before the path becomes muddy and slippery or you may end up in the water! From here you will get a great view down the river, with the bridge now high over your head.

42. Turn right and follow Coronation Road to **Vauxhall Bridge (30)**. Cross Vauxhall Bridge and its extension over Cumberland Road. Walk west downstream along the right hand side of Cumberland Road. At the intersection with Avon Crescent, cross Cumberland road to the left side. In 50m fork left along the Metrobus lane past one of the three huge redbrick Tobacco Bond warehouses (early 1900s) to **Ashton Avenue Bridge (31)**.
Here there are a good views downstream of Avon Bridge and in the distance the Clifton Suspension Bridge.

43. Cross Ashton Avenue Bridge and turn right to follow the path on the edge of Ashton Gate Park downstream to **Avon Bridge (32)**.

44. Pass underneath the bridge and then use the stairs or the ramp on the left to reach road

level. Cross the Avon on the left-hand pavement of Avon Bridge, which takes you onto an exit ramp. Follow the exit ramp down to its end where on the left is the **South Entrance Lock Bridge (33)**. Cross the bridge.

As you cross the bridge, the Plimsoll Bridge looms above you on the right, just beyond is a concrete walkway you will cross shortly, and in the distance you can see New Junction Lock and its swing bridge.

45. Pass through the metal railings and turn right (past Brunel's Swivel Bridge on the dockside on your left), then walk anticlockwise around the central pivot of the Plimsoll Bridge.

Howards Entrance Lock (1873) is on your left and the water of Cumberland Basin (1809) is straight ahead.

46. In a few metres you reach the **South Entrance Lock Walkway (34)**. Cross this concrete walkway.

47. In a few metres, turn right just after the giant anchor, to cross the grass, then turn right along Brunel Lock Road. Pass beneath **Plimsoll Bridge(35)** then use the spiral stairs on the right to climb up to road level. Turn left and cross the bridge. On the far side take the stairs down again.

As you cross the bridge, below you there is a good view of Brunel's Entrance Lock (1849). To the right of this is the now truncated entrance to Jessop's original Entrance Lock (1809), and to the right again, Howards Entrance Lock (1873).

48. At the bottom of the stairs, immediately left there are four little steps and an open gate through which we pass onto the street pavement. Turn left, and in 100m go onto the footbridge and use it to cross Hotwells Road to Granby Hill

49. Follow Granby Hill upwards until it ends at the grand Royal York Crescent and becomes York Gardens.

Royal York Crescent dates from 1791–1820 and comprises 46 houses, possibly designed by William Paty.

50. Follow York Gardens up to the left which takes us onto Wellington Terrace which then becomes Sion Hill.

At the end of Wellington Terrace is the Avon Gorge Hotel, followed by the entrance arch of the former Clifton Rocks Railway, which was a funicular railway that ran from here down to the Portway. It ran from 1893 –1934, and during WWII it was a secret tranmission base for the BBC.

51. Cross to the Clifton Rocks Railway side and take the path to the left to reach the **Clifton Suspension Bridge (36)** and cross the bridge.

Just over the bridge is Burwalls on the left and the Bridge Visitor Centre on the right. Burwalls was built in 1872 for local newspaper proprietor Joseph Leech, designed by local architects Foster and Wood. In 1897, it became the family home of George Wills, tobacco baron. In 1946, it was bought by Bristol University. In 2016, it was converted into luxury apartments.

The excellent Bridge Visitor Centre is open every day, with free entry.

52. Turn right into North Road.

Nightingale Valley is on the right and there are excellent views across the gorge of the tower of Clifton Observatory (1766) which houses a Camera Obscura. Half way down the cliff is the observation platform of the "Giants Cave".

53. When North Road dips slightly, enter Leigh Woods through a gate on the right. We recommend that you take a phone pic of the map on the Information board. You now follow route 41 all the way through Leigh Woods. Walk uphill on the leftmost path. 200m after the Rangers hut turn left through a gap in the wall — signposted.

54. 500m after the gap in the wall you reach a tarmac road. Turn right. After 300m the road bends slightly to the left and a sign directs you gently downhill towards Paradise Bottom. 1.5km after this sign, watch out for another signpost on the left side of the track. Turn sharp right here on Route 41 towards Pill. You emerge from Leigh Woods at an elevated point overlooking the river. Turn left and head downhill. You will pass a railway viaduct on the left for the Portishead line.

Over the water you will eventually have a view of the Sea Mills railway bridge. Immediately behind it, across the tributary of the Trym, are the ruined walls of a wet dock dating from 1712. Immediately behind that you have a fine view of the Portway Viaduct (1926) which you will cross later. To the left of the Portway, in the middle distance, is the tower of St Ediths (1924). Further on you pass the low cliffs of the Avon's Horseshoe Bend on the opposite bank. The cliffs are a protected site of Special Scientific Interest because of the vegetation. Horseshoe Bend was a notoriously tricky spot for large ships to steer round. In 1874, the SS Kron Prinz, containing 200 tons of grain, grounded on the outer bank. The ship settled onto the steep mud bank and then tipped over. The cargo of grain was lost. Eventually, the ship was refloated and taken to Bristol for expensive repairs.

55. At Chapel Pill Farm, keep straight onto the tarmac road which becomes Chapel Pill Lane. Pass Ham Green Fishing Lakes on the left. At the end of Chapel Pill Lane, carry on in a straight line across the green, then dog-leg right and left and go across Watchouse Hill — probably the sit of an Iron Age hillfort.

56. At Pill Sports Field, you will reach a cycle route 41 sign on a low post. At this point veer off the path to the right. Keep the netball pitch on your left and head towards the hedge. A pair of white grain elevators at Avonmouth should be directly ahead in the far distance.

From here you will get a splendid view of the Avonmouth Road Bridge which you will cross shortly.

57. Drop down towards the bottom corner of the field, keeping the hedge on your right. Here a small gap/stile leads you into a lane in front of cottages. At the bottom of this lane turn left towards into the village of Pill (two pubs!) and walk all the way around the inlet, passing under the railway viaduct, and turn left into Marine Parade.

Pill (meaning inlet or harbour) was traditionally the residence of pilots who would guide boats up the Avon Gorge, between the Bristol Channel and the Port of Bristol.

58. After 150m, as Marine Parade turns to the

WALK INSTRUCTIONS | **141**

left, continue straight on up a few steps onto the grassed ridge of the flood defences. Follow the ridge around a sharp left turn, then a sharp right turn, and keep to the right of the houses.

59. At a stile in a wooden fence, climb over onto the tarmac cycleway, turn right and proceed onwards, upwards and over **Avonmouth Bridge (37)**.

60. After crossing the Avon, at a gap in the barrier on your right, take the steps down to ground level. Walk straight along the line of the bridge and across a small grassed area until you reach the junction of the Portway with West Town Road. Turn left and cross over the Portway at the traffic lights. Turn right, cross to the pavement on West Town Road. Continue down West Town Road.

61. Just after the railway line, cross over and take the signposted footpath into Lamplighters Marsh Nature Reserve and go through the metal entranceway. After 30m or so you will come to an interpretation board.
You have now joined the final leg of the Severn Way, a 338km long-distance path from the source of the River Severn at Plynlimon, in the uplands of mid-Wales to Bristol. For a two-minute diversion to the water's edge, and well worth it, at the interpretation board, head off the path at not quite 90 degrees towards the nearest bridge support pillar. You will soon see a gap in the thicket. Walk down this path for 30m and you will emerge in a clearing on the river bank with fine views up and down the river.

62. Take the path through the nature reserve until you reach the former Pill Ferry slipway and the historic Lamplighters Pub, which dates from 1760.
It was at this spot that King William III (William of Orange) landed in July 1690, on his return to England after defeating James II in the Battle of the Boyne in Ireland. The battle marked the end of James' efforts to wrest the English Crown back from the Dutch Invader. King William spent a night at nearby Kings Weston House.

63. Take the footpath ahead signposted to Sea Mills. Keep to the right hand edge of the sports fields.
Across the river you will soon see a white building with two squat towers and an arch. This is known as the Ham Green Folly, and was probably a watergate for nearby Ham Green House. In the 1920s, two nurses sunbathing near there were swept away by the wake of a passing ship and drowned.

64. When the riverside path ends, turn left into Northleach Road, then immediately right into Woodwell Road.

65. Cross the little concrete railway bridge and immediately take the path to the right. After 400m, at the top of some steps, you will have a superb view looking down onto Horseshoe Bend of the River Avon. As you reach two metal gates continue on the path signed to Sea Mills.

66. After another 500m you will see sports fields ahead and when the path forks, take the right hand fork.

67. 100m beyond the fork, the path turns right under a railway bridge. In 1 km you arrive at Sea Mills. Pass under the railway bridge.
Sea Mills was a Roman settlement, called Portus Abonae, abandoned by the 4th century AD. The substantial stone walls in the channel of the River Trym, immediately to your right, are the remains of a wet dock built in 1712 by Joshua Franklyn, a Bristol merchant, to eliminate the need for large sailing ships to navigate the tricky route of the River Avon any further upstream. However, it never thrived due to poor transport links and was in disrepair by the end of the 18th century.

68. Now pass underneath the **Portway Viaduct (38)**.
For a pleasant short diversion and a splendid view of this beautiful bridge, carry straight on northwards along the bank of the Trym for 300m and cross over it by means of the little Trym Cross Bridge. Now walk south and return to the route by crossing over the little concrete footbridge on the north side of the viaduct.

69. Walk up the slope and cross the Portway Viaduct. The pavement across the bridge is very narrow, so take care here, although there is a cycle lane between you and the traffic. Turn left into Roman Way.
Where Roman Way joins the Portway are the remains of a Roman villa probably dating from the third century, which was part of the Roman settlement of Portus Abonae.

70. Walk up Sabrina Way for a few metres then turn right into Horse Shoe Drive. At the end of the drive take the steps down a few metres to another path and turn left. In 15m, take the right hand path at a fork and zig-zag down to the bottom of the slope and pass through a stile into Old Sneed Park Nature Reserve.

71. Keep to the right along the edge of the field and go through a gate into Bishops Knoll. Walk up the hill to another gate and turn left and continue up the hill to Bramble Lane.

72. At Bramble Lane, turn right and then keep straight on up Knoll Hill, followed by Seawalls Road. Turn left into The Avenue, then first right into Ivywell Road.

73. At the junction with Circular Road, turn right and carry on until it joins Ladies Mile. Turn right down Fountain Hill, following the raised footpath on your right. At the road junction ahead cross over the top of Bridge Valley Road to the Promenade.

74. Follow the wide footpath which directs you to the Clifton Suspension Bridge. After 400m, fork right to follow the public footpath sign. Take this path up and around (with glorious views of the gorge, river and bridge) to pass in front of the Observatory. Continue to follow this path as it now winds down to meet the junction of Observatory Road and Gloucester Row. Turn left along Gloucester Row to reach a zebra crossing. Cross over to turn down the Mall.

75. Follow the Mall to its end and turn left onto Princess Victoria street and follow it to its end.
As you walk down the Mall, on your left, opposite the Mall Gardens, you pass No 22, The Clifton

Assembly Rooms, with a very imposing Grade II Classical facade of 1811 with six giant half-columns. It was designed by Bristol architect Francis Greenway, who was convicted of forgery in 1812 and sentenced to death, later commuted to transport to Australia, where he became the first Government Architect. Greenway's face was shown on the first Australian $10 note (1966–93), making him probably the only convicted forger in the world to be honoured on a banknote.

76. At the end of the Mall, turn right onto Regent Street, and follow it to its intersection with Hensman's Hill where it becomes Clifton Hill. After 30m on Clifton Hill take a small path on the right which leads steeply downwards.

77. The path leads to Goldney Avenue where you turn right and then immediately left (and down) onto Goldney Road.

78. Follow Goldney Road to its end, which is a dead end for cars but not for walkers. Turn right onto the lane to go further down the hill. Note the fine distant views. The lane ends on Ambra Vale, where you continue straight and follow it down to Hotwells Road.

79. Turn right onto Hotwells Road and cross over via the traffic island to the opposite side of Hotwells Road. Take the second right into Rownham Mead.

80. Ahead of you, you will see a metal archway leading to Poole's Wharf Court. Pass under the archway and continue straight on through a gap between the houses. Pass through a metal gate and enjoy a surprise return to the harbourside. Turn right and follow the harbourside path.
In 50 m you pass a wide gap in the harbour wall which was the former entrance to the huge Merchants/Champion's Wet Dock (1773) which survived until 1967.

81. Cross **Poole's Wharf bridge (39)** and carry straight on, past the Pump House Pub to **New Junction Lock Bridge (40)**. Turn left and cross the bridge.
The shiny curved corrugated metal cabins that flank the bridge house the control rooms and pumps that open the lock gates and the bridge.

82. Go straight on to cross **Old Junction Lock Bridge (41)**. Continue straight ahead into Avon Crescent. After 100m, meters you carry on along Cumberland Road. In 50m, turn left into Underfall Yard.
The redbrick buildings on your left as you turn into the yard house the control systems for the sluice gates (underground beneath you) that control the level of the water in the Floating Harbour.

83. Turn right at the water.
You shortly pass the Cottage Pub (1868) which used to be used for storage of timber, and was the Harbourmasters Office (1975–83). There is a good view across the basin to Poole's Wharf Bridge.

84. At Bristol Marina turn right (no option!) then left across the head of the Marina. In 100m turn right into Hannover Place, and after 100m, turn left to follow the harbourside walkway. Pass the former Albion Dock on your left.
Albion Dock (1820) was the largest dry dock in Bristol, created by Charles Hill and James Hilhouse, who built many ships on the site until 1977. Abels Shipbuilders occupied it 1980–2016.

85. At Gas Ferry Road turn left.
The head office of Aardman Animations, creators of Wallace and Gromit, is straight ahead before you make the turn.

86. In 100m turn right to walk along the Harbour again for 500m.

87. At Prince's Wharf turn left to cross **Prince Street Bridge (42)**, then turn left again until you reach John Cabot's statue in front of Bush House. Turn right and follow St Augustine's Reach along Narrow Quay to **Pero's Bridge (43)**.

88. Turn left to cross Pero's Bridge then immediately turn right and follow the water to the point where it disappears beneath the waterfall. Turn right and cross the head of St Augustine's Reach to Broad Quay.
St Augustine's Reach used to extend northwards for a further 250m but was covered over in the 1930s to create "The Centre". It used to be the heart of the Port of Bristol — crowded with tall-masted ocean-going ships.

89. Turn right along Broad Quay for 100m until it meets Prince Street, then cross over and walk ahead into Queen Square. Cross diagonally through Queen Square.
Queen Square is one of the finest Georgian squares in the country, named after Queen Anne, who visited the city in 1702. It was extensively damaged by fire in the Bristol Corn Law riots of 1831. The equestrian statue of William III, in the centre of the square, is by John Michael Rysbrack, cast in 1733, and is one of the best of its kind in Europe.

90. Exit Queen Square past the Hole in the Wall pub (probably 17th or 18th century) keeping left to cross **Redcliffe Bridge (44)**.
As you approach Redciffe Bridge the cathedral-sized St Mary Redcliffe Church (mostly 13th and 14th century) is behind it in the middle distance.

91. Straight after the bridge, turn left onto the waterside path which, in 50m, turns right. Dog-leg to the left along Redcliffe Back and Ferry Street to turn left into Redcliffe Street. Take the first right into Thomas Lane, and pass the historic Seven Stars Pub (note the plaque on the wall). Turn left onto St Thomas Street.

92. At Victoria Street turn right and immediately cross over into Counterslip.

93. Take the first left turn into Old Temple Street, which brings you to a small square. Folllow the path around the building straight ahead and you will reach **Castle Bridge (45)**, the final bridge in the walk.

94. Cross Castle Bridge into Castle Park. Give yourself a pat on the back — you have now walked over all of Bristol's 45 bridges, crossing each one only once! To return to your starting point, turn left and walk 300m to Bristol Bridge.

WALK INSTRUCTIONS | 143

SELECTED BIBLIOGRAPHY

Baker, N., Brett, J., Jones, R., *Bristol: A Worshipful Town and Famous City: An Archaeological Assessment* Oxbow Books 2018

Backwith, D., Ball, R., Hunt, S. E., Richardson, M. *Strikers, Hobblers, Conchies and Reds A Radical History of Bristol 1880–1939* Breviary Stuff Publications 2014

Bristol City Council *Bristol Harbour Heritage Trail* 2009

Benbrook, I. *Bristol City Docks A Guide to the Historic Harbour* Redcliffe Press 1989

Binding, J. *Brunel's Bristol Temple Meads* Oxford Publishing Co 2001

Bishop, J. *Bristol Through Maps* Redcliffe Press 2016

Dresser, M., Ollerenshaw, P. *The Making of Modern Bristol* Redcliffe Press 1996

Foyle, A. *Pevsners Architectural Guides: Bristol* Yale University Press 2004

Harrison, D. *The Bridges of Mediaeval England: Transport and Society 400–1800* Oxford University Press 2010

Kelly, A., Kelly, M., *Brunel: In Love with the Impossible* Bristol Cultural Development Partnership 2006

Lewis, B. *Bristol City Docks Through Time* Amberley Publishing 2009

Malpass, P. and King, A. *Bristol's Floating Harbour: The First 200 Years* Redcliffe Press 2009

Manson, M. *Riot! The Bristol Bridge Massacre of 1793* Past and Present Press 1997

Manson, M. *Bristol Beyond the Bridge* Redcliffe Press 1988

Mowl, T. *Bristol Explored — Twelve Architectural Walks* Pub. Stephen Morris 2015

Pascoe, M. *150 Years of Clifton Suspension Bridge* The History press 2014

Penny, J. *Bristol At War* Breedon Books Publishing Company 2002

Philips, T., Davies. S, Packer, R., Davies, B. *St Philips Marsh* R P Printing Services (undated)

Ruddock, T. *Arch Bridges and Their Builders 1735–1855* Cambridge University Press 1979

Tippett, W. *Unloved Landscapes — The Bristol Schemes of Sylvia Crowe* Bristol Civic Society Magazine Issue 8 Spring 2016

Underdown, T. H. J. *Bristol Under Blitz* J W Arrowsmith Ltd. 1942

Wells, J. *A Short History of the Port of Bristol* J W Arrowsmith 1909

White K. (Ed) *A Celebration of Avon New Cut* Fiducia Press 2006

Whitefield, A. *Mr Hilhouse of Bristol* Redcliffe Press 2010

ONLINE RESOURCES

British Newspaper Archive (Online)

Know Your Place (Bristol)

ACKNOWLEDGEMENTS

Thanks go to the following people who kindly provided, or checked, some of the facts and information which found its way into this book.

Andy King, Senior Collections Officer, M Shed, Bristol City Council; Peter Insole and David Martyn, City Design Group (Urban Design) Bristol City Council; Archive Staff, SS Great Britain; Staff of Bristol City Reference Library; Geoff Booth, director, Codorus Engineering Ltd; Hector Beade-Pereda, associate, Knight Architects; Nick Childs, director, Childs Sulzmann Architects; Tim King, director, WSP; Ian Johnson, engineer, Bristol City Docks; Peter Read, Knowle and Totterdown Local History Society; Alan Tully, contracts manager, John Sisk & Son Ltd; Martin Kendall, director, The Bush Consultancy; Hannah Little, archivist, Clifton Suspension Bridge Trust; Níall McLaughlin, director, Níall McLaughlin Architects; Gerry Nicholls; Geoff Gudge, engineer, formerly of HLD Ltd, Darren Dancey, Managing Director, Crest Nicholson South West; Bristol Then and Now Questions Facebook Page members; Bristol Industrial Archaeology Society Facebook Page members.

Finally, special thanks to Professor Tim Mowl, without whom this book would not have been started, and to Bristol University for their generous sponsorship.